BICYCLING
A REINTRODUCTION

A VISUAL GUIDE TO CHOOSING, REPAIRING, MAINTAINING & OPERATING A BICYCLE

KAREN RUTH

Creative Publishing
international

Creative Publishing international

Library of Congress Cataloging-in-Publication Data

Ruth, Karen.
 Bicycling, a reintroduction : a visual guide to choosing,
repairing, maintaining & operating a bicycle /
by Karen Ruth.
    p. cm.
 Includes index.
 ISBN-13: 978-1-58923-604-2 (soft cover)
 ISBN-10: 1-58923-604-1 (soft cover)
 1. Cycling. 2. Bicycles--Equipment and supplies.
 3. Bicycles--Maintenance and repair. I. Title.
 GV1041.R87 2011
 388.3'472--dc22
                                    2011000818

President/CEO: Ken Fund

Home Improvement Group

Publisher: Bryan Trandem
Managing Editor: Tracy Stanley
Senior Editor: Mark Johanson
Creative Director: Michele Lanci-Altomare
Art Direction/Design: Brad Springer, Kim Winscher,
    James Kegley
Lead Photographer: Joel Schnell
Set Builder: James Parmeter
Production Managers: Laura Hokkanen, Linda Halls

Author: Karen Ruth
Page Layout Artist: Kathleen Littfin
Tech Editor: Cole Perry
Photo Tech: Karen Ruth

Thanks to all the Twin Cities' area local bike shop owners
and managers who assisted in the creation of this book.

Very special thanks to Bill Berger and Joan Kahle-Berger of
Gateway Cycle (gatewaycycle.com) for loaning bikes and
product, modeling for photos, and allowing us to use their
retail space as a photo studio. Special thanks also to Gene
Oberpriller at One on One Bicycle Gallery (oneononebike.
com) for letting us monopolize their sales area while
shooting photos. Thank you to Martin Erickson at County
Cycles (countycycles.com) for loan of the bike trailer.

Thanks also to Erik's Bike Shop (eriksbikeshop.com) and
Calhoun Cycle (calhouncycle.com) for allowing us to
photograph their retail spaces. Thanks to Marcy Levine at
Freewheel Bike (freewheelbike.com) for her willingness to
answer every cycling question I have ever had for the past
twenty years.

Finally, thanks to Peg Baier for teaching me to spin and
draft while pedaling around France.

Contents

Introduction

Perhaps you haven't ridden a bike since you were twelve, and now you want to hit the road again. Maybe your knees are sore from running, and you want to find another outdoor exercise to enjoy. Or you feel that it is silly to start up the car to drive a mile to the grocery store or the transit stop. Your colleagues are showing up to work with bright eyes and rosy cheeks after having biked in on a beautiful morning, and you're wondering whether you could do the same thing.

If so, this book is for you!

This book is for you if you haven't ridden in years and are wondering what's new in cycling. This book is for you if you want to explore a different way to get a good aerobic workout. Want to start shopping or commuting by bike? This book is for you.

Bicycling: A Reintroduction covers all the basics you need to hop back on your bike after years away. How to buy a new bike that fits your body and your needs is covered. All the baffling styles and trends on display at the bike shop will be explained, so you can determine how best to match your cycling needs to one of those shiny new machines. If you aren't in the market for a new bike, how to evaluate your current bike or find a quality used bike is discussed.

Tips and tricks for becoming a competent, efficient rider are offered. Safety and security concerns are addressed.

If you are a beginning biker but are curious about what is out there to challenge you and improve your skills and increase your fun, a chapter is devoted to moving beyond the basics.

Finally, a number of basic fix-it tasks are covered, so you can take care of flat tires, cranky shifters, and dirty chains.

The world of bicycling has changed a lot since the days when the Schwinn Sting Ray ruled the playground. Your modern bicycle won't have a banana seat or a gear shifter on the sissy bar, but if you stay out riding past curfew you probably won't get grounded.

CHAPTER 1

Why Bike? Why Now?

In the 1880s and '90s the bicycle was enormously popular in America and Europe. The advent of the auto was decades away, and bicycles were cheaper, faster, and cleaner than horses. Composers wrote popular music featuring the bicycle. Bicycling clubs lobbied for paved roads. The pneumatic tire was patented for bicycle use. Even Susan B. Anthony lauded the bicycle as one of the most important advancements for women's freedom. The advent of bloomers and the demise of the bustle were directly tied to the popularity of cycling for women.

But what happened? In America, the automobile, two world wars, urbanization—all played a role in pushing the bicycle from a highly touted adult vehicle to a toy for child's play.

Fortunately, we have come back around to excitement about cycling, perhaps not full circle, but partially. More bike styles are available in more price ranges and more sizes. Cycling organizations are lobbying for more bicycle services, and more bicycle access. We can all benefit from the resurgence in cycling popularity.

Americans are, perhaps, beginning to see that bicycles are a legitimate transportation tool, and not simply a toy or piece of athletic equipment.

The time to bike is now.

Adult-Size Bicycles Sold in the U.S. (In Millions)

Year	Units Sold
2008	13.4
2003	12.9
1998	11.1
1993	13
1988	9.9
1983	9
1973	15.2

SOURCE: National Bicycle Dealers Association

After reaching an all-time high of 15.2 million adult bicycles (20" wheel and larger) sold in 1973, sales volume fell off a bit in the U.S., only to rebound nicely in the past five years. Currently, the U.S. bicycle industry is estimated at $6 billion.

● MORE BIKE CHOICES

Today, you'll find more equipment options than ever before. Unlike the 1970s, when your only bike choices were the 10-speed road bike or an upright 3-speed, or the 1990s when mountain bikes were the hot item, we now have many, many choices combining the best configurations for a variety of activities.

Fortunately, someone caught on to the fact that most of us aren't road racers. Comfort bikes are now widely made. Bikes with chain guards and easy riding positions are now made so we don't get dirty and cramped up on our way to the park. Racks, packs, and trailers make carting groceries or the kids much easier. Super low gearing means that it is easier to pull the kids' trailer or ride up those hills.

You can buy a folding bike that, in just ten seconds, knocks down to the size of a large briefcase. Ride to the train, fold up your bike, and hop on. You can buy bikes or bike extenders that allow you to bike to the beach with your surfboard. You can find bikes in any price range and through a variety of outlets. If you want, you can get your hands dirty and do all your own maintenance and repair. You don't need fancy electronics to diagnose bike problems, and with a few exceptions, if you have even moderate mechanical aptitude, you can fix most common bike problems. On the other hand, if you never want to think about bike maintenance, there are options that are pretty close to worry free.

If you want a cargo bike that can haul your purchases home from the hardware store, you can get that too. Need help with those pesky hills? An electric assist bike can give you the extra boost you need. How about a bike that is yours in every dimension? Custom builders like Bespoke Cycles of San Francisco will, for a price, create whatever you want.

Need a little more oomph to get up those hills? An electric bike has power at the ready.

Folding bikes offer a comfortable ride while taking up less space for the ultimate in portability.

MORE RIDING OPTIONS

With more and more auto traffic on the roads, it's important that some headway has been made in creating bike friendly routes. Federal highway dollars are now linked to increasing pedestrian and cycling options along with road building projects. This may include better signage, wider shoulders, or dedicated bike paths. We also have more places to ride. Railroad rights-of-way have been converted to bike trails all over the country. According to the organization Rails to Trails, there are nearly 20,000 miles of rail trails currently available, with almost 10,000 miles of potential routes in the works. These trails range from rough gravel trails suitable for mountain bike use to asphalt paved trails that any bike can use. The great thing about rail trails? Most rail beds are graded at less than 2 percent, so all the climbs are long and gradual.

Cities and towns are also making great strides in improving cycling options. Dedicated cycling lanes and pathways are showing up all over the place. Maps of good cycling routes are available for almost every urban area. Google Maps now has a biking option. In some urban areas you can rent a bike for short trips from a street kiosk. Bicycle rental for a day or week of sightseeing is available in most tourist areas.

Even something as simple as a sign can greatly increase safety for bicyclists.

More and more cities offer short term rental bikes available at kiosks spread throughout downtown areas. The Nice Ride program, for example, is co-sponsored by the city of Minneapolis and a health care organization.

Great bicycling trails and commuter routes are being built all over.

• MORE HEALTH BENEFITS

Bicycling is a healthy choice. You typically burn more calories cycling at a slow pace than you do walking at a slow pace. And you cover more ground! You generate your own breeze, so you don't get as warm. It's a great way to save on gas, which of course is beneficial for the environment.

Bicycling is much less jarring on your body and easier on your knees than jogging. Many people cycle well into old age—in fact, if you ride a supported cross-country bike tour, the average rider age is around 60.

Bicyclists are more connected to their surroundings. Without climate control and windows to roll up, the cyclist feels every nuance of wind and temperature. And also every bump in the road. Psychological studies have found that time out of doors is a great mood enhancer. Exercise out of doors is more effective at mood stabilization than exercise indoors.

If you can commute, even partially, by bicycle, you will soon come to relish the happiness that biking home can bring. By the time you arrive at your doorstep, the worries of the day are behind you. You have filled your lungs with oxygen and pumped your blood around to burn off stress—much better than sitting in the outbound lane for thirty minutes.

If you wish, you can choose from many cycling organizations to join if you don't want to bike alone. Socializing with like-minded people is also a health booster.

Bicycling is a lifelong sport and it can be a healthful form of social networking.

Ride to the train, fold up the bike, ride the train to the city, unfold the bike—it's point-to-point without waiting or walking.

● MORE ROOM TO GROW

One of the beauties of cycling is that you can be as casual or as serious a rider as you desire. You can cruise around the neighborhood for 20 minutes, or cycle across the country in 60 days. (Yes, that's all the time it takes to ride from coast to coast.) Bicycle tours come in all shapes and sizes in all parts of the world. Cycling is an excellent way to play tourist—you can see more out-of-the-way places and experience an area's true back road nature. You can purchase luxury packages complete with catered meals and beautiful accommodations, or you can rough it and camp. Mountain biking is a wonderful way to see more of our country's outdoor areas while having a whiz-bang good time.

Cycling is an excellent way to tour an area. Because cycle tourists are more likely to frequent back roads, they experience the unique qualities of an area, rather than the urban build up that is remarkably similar regardless of what country you are in. Or bicycling can be combined with car, RV, or boat travel. Many national and state parks have paved bike paths or low-speed-limit parkways that are perfect for fully enjoying the beauty of the area.

Clubs and charities regularly sponsor rides and tours of all sorts. In some cities, streets are closed to motor traffic along a route for a day or weekend. Many clubs sponsor century (100 mile) rides on summer weekends. At least forty states have a multi-day supported ride, and more are added every year.

If you have a competitive nature, you can join a cycling club or team and hone your speed and riding technique with team rides and races. Like running, there are age group and level categories, so you compete against people at a similar level.

There is stunning scenery within view of many bike-accessible trails.

Bringing along a bike adds to the variety of any vacation.

• GET A BIKE

Have you been in a bike shop recently? The choices available to cyclists are greater than ever. Bicycle manufacturers are catering to more riders and more riding styles, which creates an absolutely overwhelming number of possibilities. The good news about the various choices is that almost any rider can find exactly what he or she needs.

Bicycles are wonderful machines and delightful transport tools. But any simplicity flies out the window when you walk into a bike shop. The salesperson is excited to rattle off lists of features and advancements in frame geometry and suspension gizmos. Soon your head is filled with specs and prices and gear ratios and you forget why you are really there. It's easy to do. Most bike shops don't employ casual bike riders, because repeat customers are typically cyclists—serious riders who often consider cycling to be their lifestyle. Cyclists want to talk to other cyclists when they go to buy cycling paraphernalia.

If you are a casual rider it is important to find a bike shop that understands or caters to your style. The shops are out there; you just need to find the one that is right for you.

Large bike shops will stock hundreds and even thousands of machines, so it pays to do a little planning and research before you start to browse.

Finding a Bike Shop

If you are purchasing a new bike, take the time upfront to find a bike shop that suits your needs. In a metropolitan area this may be easy, as bike shops have been springing up all over. In rural areas you may have to travel a bit, but the trip will be worth it. Once you have determined what style rider you are and what type of riding you will be doing, take the time to research the bike shops in your area. Some shops specialize in racing bikes. If you want a cruise around the neighborhood kind of bike, you will not be happy in this kind of shop. Other shops specialize in recumbents—if you aren't looking for a recumbent you won't be happy with this choice. Check out websites or make a few phone calls to start. Also, ask your friends, neighbors, or strangers about their bike shop. If you see someone riding a bike that looks appealing to you, ask about it. Cyclists generally enjoy sharing information, and you can learn a lot from being a little nosy and outgoing.

All bikes arrive at retailers partially assembled. At a professional bike shop, an experienced mechanic will assemble the bike and test ride it. Then, the bike will be adjusted to fit you correctly.

Many bike shops specialize in a few brands or a particular form of bicycle. This shop is known for recumbents and folding bikes.

Buying Online

What about buying a bike online? If you check out the websites for major bike manufacturers, you will see that most do not sell their bikes online. Bike manufacturers understand that personal interactions and test rides are crucial to satisfactory bike purchases. Some smaller bike manufacturers do sell online, because they have not built a network of sellers or they sell so few bikes no bike shop wants to carry the overhead of having one on hand to test ride. Many touring bikes and utility transportation bikes fall into this category. If this is the style of bike you are after, you may have to buy your bike on faith. Another option is to plan your cycling vacation around visiting the manufacturer or a shop that does carry stock. It may help to search the Internet for reviews of the bicycle, or for owners' groups. You may be able to find owners nearby who would let you inspect their bikes.

A leisurely bike ride through parklands is a wonderful way to begin or end the day. An upright bike with medium sized tires is perfect for this ride.

Big-Box Stores

What about buying a bike at a large national chain store or discount retailer? For a child's bike, this tactic makes a lot of sense. Children quickly outgrow bikes, so a two- or three-year lifespan might be all that is reasonable to expect from a kid's bike. A big box store is also an option for procuring an adult's bike, but only if he or she is planning nothing but short, leisurely and infrequent rides. An entry level, mass market bicycle will have a lifespan of about 2,000 miles. If the bike is to be used for rides around the neighborhood and an occasional longer ride on a bike trail, a value-driven choice might be best. An investment of only a hundred dollars or two also means you may not feel as guilty if your new bike stays parked in the garage for weeks on end.

There are some significant drawbacks to purchasing your bike at a big box store. Most important, you can't test-ride the bike! Fit and feel is important in cycling—buying without riding doesn't make much sense. The bike may not be returnable once the tires have rolled over pavement. The other big drawbacks are that you'll be unlikely to get useful assistance from a knowledgeable cyclist, and the bike you buy may not be repairable or modifiable. Because these bicycles are produced in very large numbers for very low cost, many parts are push-together pieces that can't be removed without destroying them.

Evaluate Your Existing Bike

You may already have a bike sitting in your garage gathering dust. Is it dusty because it was a pain to ride, or did you get busy with other parts of your life? If it was a pain to ride, move on to something different. Biking should be fun, and outright pain should be non-existent or minimal unless you are grinding out high mileage workouts.

If you can't remember how the bike felt, put some air in the tires and take it out for a spin. As you ride think about how the bike feels. Is it comfortable? Are you sitting as upright as you would like to? Do you feel too stretched out, or too scrunched up? Can you easily stand over the top bar? Does it feel like your wrists and hands are comfortable? Do you feel that you can control the bike, or does it feel unmanageable? Are the shifters and brake levers easy to reach and use? Is the seat comfy?

Some of the above issues are minor—there are many seat styles you can try to find for a more comfortable perch. However, if you feel that you are too horizontal or stretched out on the bike, or you can't comfortably stand over the top bar, then a different bike is probably in order. Donate your old bike and move on to something better.

Purchase a New Bike

Your first objective is to determine your riding style and what you will need from a bicycle to match that style.

Here are some questions to ask yourself. Think about the answers in advance so you're prepared to have a productive experience with your bike seller.

- What type of riding do you want to do?
- Will you be commuting to work and picking up groceries? Every day or once a week?
- Do you want to take a leisurely turn around the neighborhood of an evening?
- Are you interested in longer distance riding, perhaps a weekend trip on a local trail?
- What type of surfaces will you be riding on? Off road on dirt, sand, and rocks? On gravel? Paved or hard packed trails? City streets?
- Do you want to maximize physical comfort?
- Do you want to maximize speed?
- Do you need the toughest bike out there?
- How mechanically inclined are you?
- Do you need a bike that never needs any input from you, or are you willing to get your hands dirty once in a while?
- Are you concerned with appearance (it's okay if you are)? Or are you strictly interested in performance?

Riding on dirt or gravel roads requires wider, squishier tires with a little bit of tread for traction.

Rough terrain with hills to climb requires a tough mountain bike with suspension, good brakes, and knobby tires.

For speed on smooth roads, nothing beats a super light aluminum or carbon fiber road bike with skinny tires and aerodynamic features.

Riding Style and Primary Use

The style of riding you prefer has great impact on which type of bicycle will work best for you. You don't need to be down in an aerodynamic tuck on a road bike when you simply want to ride around the park. Conversely, if your goal is high-mileage workouts, that comfy, chunky cruiser is going to hold you back. Before you head to the bike shop, clarify what style rider you are, or wish to be.

How you use your bike is also an important aspect of choosing a bike, especially when it comes to gearing and accessories. If you will be transporting groceries or a change of clothes you will need racks or baskets. If you will be commuting in all sorts of weather, fenders are in order. If you want speed, you'll need lightweight components and skinny tires. Here are some categories to describe riding styles:

Leisurely—you want to be as comfortable as possible as you sit upright on a bike that feels easy-as-pie to ride. Your ideal ride is rolling around the neighborhood or along a scenic trail. The bicycle for the leisurely cruiser is the comfort style.

Casual—you want comfort for longer rides on trails or roads. You may want the option of different hand positions to accommodate for longer ride times. Your bike needs to be ready for variable road conditions and terrain. A hybrid bike is most likely the fit for the casual tourist or commuter.

Fitness—you want to challenge yourself to increasing riding time, speed, or power. You want a sturdy, yet light ride that will be comfortable on long routes over smooth surfaces. The fitness buff is well matched with a road bike.

Off-Road—you want a tough bike with the features necessary to bang down rocky, rooty trails and handle dirt, mud, or sand with ease. You need a bike that is responsive and easy to control. It's mountain bike all the way for the off-roader.

Dedicated—you really are devoted to many miles on a bike either for commuting, sport, or touring. You will eventually want multiple bikes to accommodate multiple riding styles.

Regardless of bike style, there must be a minimum of one to two inches clearance between the rider and the top tube. Stand over the bike and lift up seat and handle bars. The tires should be one to two inches off the ground before the top bar makes contact.

Bike Size

A bike needs to fit the rider. Some aspects of fit can be tweaked by adjusting seats and handlebars, but if the frame is not the proper basic size, no amount of adjusting will make it comfortable.

Standover Height—if your bike has a horizontal top tube you should be able to stand over the top tube with both feet flat on the ground. There should be an inch or two between the top bar and your crotch. Most new bikes, even road bikes, have a sloping top tube, so standover heights are now much more generous.

Length—even on a road-racing bike, which is ridden in the most down position, your elbows should always be slightly bent. Regardless of what type of bike you are riding, if you can't keep your elbows slightly bent while riding, the bike is too long.

Frame Size—bikes used to be sold by inch or centimeter frame sizes. The frame size was the length of the seat tube from the top end to the middle of the bottom bracket. Now, with most frames having slanting top tubes, this numeric measurement no longer has the same relevance. But for comparison, all the other frame components are proportional to the seat tube. That means that if you are looking at two bikes of the exact same model, the smaller frame size will have a shorter top tube. If you prefer a shorter reach, the smaller model would be better, as long as the seat post is long enough to give you a proper seat height.

Fit

Unless you're buying a high end custom bike, or are willing to shell out quite a bit of extra money, the bike you test ride at the bike shop needs to fit without modification except for raising the seat. Don't let a salesperson tell you, "You'll get used to it." If it doesn't feel good on a test ride, it won't feel good on a ten-mile ride. Take the time to test ride as many bikes as you need to. Take notes—write down the model name and a one or two word description. Bring a helmet or borrow one from the shop, and take your time riding around on the bike.

A rider on a properly sized bike will be able to ride with back straight and elbows slightly bent. The sales attendant at a pro bike shop will be happy to help you evaluate the fit.

Feel

Ride some figure eights in the parking lot (take care that you are safe from traffic). Do you feel comfortable making tight turns? Stand up and pedal. Does it feel like you have control over the bike while standing? Mount and dismount a number of times. Stop, put your feet down, and restart a number of times. Pay attention to how easy or difficult it is to shift gears and to brake. Even if it is new to you, some systems will feel more natural.

Don't be concerned about gears or brakes that seem a little out of sync or grindy. The bikes are assembled at the bike shop and adjusted, but then they may sit on the sales floor for weeks. New bike cables have a break-in period during which they must be regularly adjusted. It is not uncommon to take a new bike for a spin and have the gears not work right. Ask them to make an adjustment, and take the bike out again. If you are testing a road bike, try to incorporate a hill or two into your test ride if possible. This will give you a feel for how the bike handles under pressure.

Price

Always a sticking point, price is. Remember that a quality bike can easily last twenty to fifty years—or even longer—with proper maintenance and consistent parts availability. The upfront costs may seem prohibitive, but your ongoing costs will be smaller, especially if you choose to do much of the standard maintenance yourself. Unless you ride in very harsh conditions or put thousands of miles on your bike, you'll only need to overhaul the bike every other year or so.

All that said, be prepared for some sticker shock if you haven't been to a bike shop recently. You may recall having paid $150 for your blue Schwinn Traveler, but that was

Your test rides are important. Take your time and really get a feel for the bike. Before leaving the shop, make sure you understand the braking and shifting features of the bike.

three decades ago and bikes have changed as much as you have. If you are going to ride consistently, and ride more than a thousand miles a year, expect to spend at least $1,000 on a well-selected, quality bicycle.

Take a Test Ride

So you've found a bike shop you like, and you're pretty clear about what type of bike you want to purchase. You're at the shop and it's time to test out a few models that are in your price range. What do you look for on a test ride? First, if you haven't ridden a new bike in ten or twenty years, you will be amazed at the braking power of the new brake styles. The wonder of indexed shifting will also have you clicking through the gears with a smile on your face. Yes, the new bikes are slick, but stop drooling and pay attention to fit and feel.

Before leaving the shop, make sure you understand how the gear shifters work if you aren't familiar with the current styles. Grip and thumb shifters are fairly straight forward, but the integrated brake shifters on road bikes come in many different styles. And don't forget, the brakes work really well.

Used Bikes

If you live in an area with lots of cyclists, you may be able to find the perfect used bicycle. Some cycle shops take trade-ins, which they tune up and sell. Bike swaps are a regular annual event in some areas. Search for local bike swaps on the Internet, or ask at a shop or bike club. You may find just the bike you want at a garage sale, a used merchandise store, police auctions, or on an Internet site like Craigslist. While you can certainly find working bikes for $50 or less, high quality bikes, even if they are twenty or thirty years old, are still going to cost two or three hundred dollars unless the seller is naïve about bike values.

If going to a bike shop can be overwhelming, shopping for a used bike can be time-consuming and frustrating. Consider how valuable your time is before you spend hours trolling through Internet site bike listings looking for "the one." To speed your quest, search based on brand names or styles. Skip over any listings that don't have a picture of the actual bike that's for sale (a screen grab of a similar bike from the manufacturer's website doesn't count).

Some tips for getting a good used bike: Make sure the bike you are looking at fits your needs and isn't just a great deal. It also needs to fit you. An ill-fitting bike won't be a good deal at any price. Find a friend who has more biking knowledge than you do and ask them what they think about your potential used bike purchase. And test ride the bike!

Adding up the costs of bringing a used bike up to good, safe working condition may negate all savings on purchase price. At minimum, discount prices, two new tires and tubes cost $60, new brake and derailleur cables, $20, and labor will cost at least $80 in any market. That doesn't account for bearing adjustment, greasing, or replacing, which adds another $100 to $200. A cheap used bike is a great learning adventure if you aspire to be your own bike mechanic. But it can also be a money pit.

FOR SALE
Hybrid cruiser. Marin San Rafael 6 years old. 15 in. aluminum frame. 24 speeds, suspension fork, alloy rims. Newer tires. Good shape. $175 o.b.o 555-4626

Hundreds of used bikes can be located for sale in your area at any given time. It's up to you to decide if saving some money is worth the risk of buying an unknown.

A Note about Comfort

It is important to remember that cycling is an athletic endeavor. It involves exertion. A bike can be fitted properly, but some riders will still come back to the bike shop and say, "I'm not comfortable riding uphill!" Well, most cyclists aren't "comfortable" riding uphill—it's hard work! There are some aspects of cycling that will be uncomfortable, even on a perfectly fitting bike. Rear ends get sore, legs wear out, and hands get tired, especially if you haven't ridden in years, are out of shape, or are riding long miles. Pain from cycling can also stem from posture issues or poor riding technique (see Bicycling Posture, page 26 and Aches and Pains, page 41).

• BICYCLE GALLERY

Following are photos and descriptions of some common types of bicycles like those you'll see at your local bike shop, along with a few bikes that you can find at specialty shops. The category names are based on current conventions, but regional variations exist and in some cases bikes may possess characteristics of more than one category, making them a little tricky to describe. The models shown were selected to represent a full range of the available types and not for promotional purposes. Work with your local bike professional to select a model and brand that makes sense for you.

Road Bikes

This bike is commonly referred to as a 10-speed, even though it has been a generation since they had only ten speeds. A road bike typically means a bike with: drop handlebars; 27 inch (700 mm) diameter tires; front and rear derailluers; 8 to 11 sprockets on the cassette; usually 2 but sometimes 3 chainrings; and caliper brakes. The tires range from medium to super skinny widths, depending on whether the bike is used for touring, commuting, or racing. Road bikes are available with frames made of aluminum, steel, carbon fiber, or titanium. As the name suggests, road bikes are meant for fast riding on smooth, paved surfaces.

Mountain Bikes

The mountain bike is designed for riding on rough trails made of dirt or gravel. To facilitate this, the tires are wide (called fat tires) and may have heavy or knobby tread. The bike frame is smaller to allow for greater standover height. The bike may have shock-absorbing suspension to smooth the ride and provide greater control. The suspension may be on the front fork only, or the bike may be fully suspended, which means both front and rear wheels have suspension. The handlebars are straight bars. Shifting is done with either a grip shift or thumb shift. Brake levers are stubby with a short reach so you can easily ride with two fingers on the brakes, and brakes are cantilever, linear pull, or disc styles to provide greater stopping power and more clearance for mud.

Road bike

Mountain bike

Hybrid Bikes

A hybrid bike is one that combines features of the mountain bike and the road bike in an easy-to-ride package. The frame is usually smaller, with a slanting top tube, like a mountain bike. The handlebars are also usually the flat, mountain style bars, with twist or thumb shifters. The wheels and tires, however, are narrower and smoother than mountain bikes to make for easier riding on smooth surfaces. Brakes are usually cantilever or linear pull style, to provide for greater clearance and better braking power.

Hybrid bike

Comfort Bikes

A comfort bike features an upright riding position usually with curved handlebars. The seat is cushy and the tires are wide to provide a soft ride. The seat post may have suspension to further dampen bumps in the road, and the front fork may have suspension as well. Comfort bikes usually have triple chainrings to provide lots of gear choices.

Comfort bike

Cruisers

These bikes may also be called beach bikes. They often are single speed with a coaster brake, though many have gears and hand brakes. Cruisers feature swept back handlebars, and usually are configured so the rider can have both feet flat on the ground while seated. These bikes have big cushy tires so they can easily ride over sand and gravel.

Commuter Bikes

A commuter bike may feature an upright riding position, or may have a more horizontal riding position. The frame is fairly tough. Tires are medium wide to provide some cushion, but narrow enough to allow for good speed. A dedicated commuter bike will come with fenders and racks installed, otherwise a commuter bike frame has attachment points (braze-ons) for this gear.

Cruiser

Commuter

Cyclocross bike

Cyclocross

A cyclocross bike is one developed for the sport of cyclocross. Cyclocross involves alternately biking across rough terrain and running while carrying the bike over obstacles. Since cyclocross is usually done in the bicycling off season (winter or rainy season) the courses are typically muddy. Or icy and snowy. A cyclocross bike looks like a road bike with drop handlebars, but the gearing is more like a mountain bike and the tires are wider and have more tread, but not as much as mountain bikes. Brakes are usually cantilever or linear pull. Many commuters choose cyclocross bikes for their daily ride.

Folding Bikes

Folding bikes are exactly that. They fold into a compact, lightweight bundle that can be easily carried by handle or carrying strap. They feature smaller diameter wheels and usually are made of lightweight aluminum. Some folders are light and compact enough to carry onto public transport, while others fold or dismantle into a bundle that easily fits into a car trunk. Coupling bikes are often full size bikes with joints in the top and down tubes so they can be folded in half.

Recumbent Bikes

A recumbent is designed so you are riding as though seated in a chair, with your legs out in front of you. There is no single standard design for recumbents. Some have a 27-inch wheel in the back and a 20-inch wheel in front. Some have two small wheels. For some the front wheel may be under the rider. The handlebars may be in front of the rider or under the seat. The major benefit of the recumbent bike is no stress is placed on the arms and hands, and the seat provides support. Recumbent tricycles are also available.

Folding bike

Recumbent bike

BMX

The BMX (bicycle motocross) is a specialty bike for trick riding or BMX track or trail riding. This bicycle has one gear, sometimes coaster brakes, and a small frame. If it has hand brakes, they are engineered so the handlebars can be spun without restriction. The wheels are usually 20-inch size. The seat is kept low so it doesn't interfere with the rider while performing tricks or jumps.

BMX bike

Fixed Gear Bikes

A fixed gear bike is a bicycle of practically any style that has one forward gear and no freewheel or coaster brake. On a fixed gear bike you can pedal forward or backward and that's the direction you go. Usually used for track racing, many urban riders have adopted this as the epitome of bicycle simplicity. This is not a bike for a casual rider, as it typically has no brake except the resistance you provide by slowing your tempo, and only has one gear, which makes hills difficult.

Fixed gear bike

Tandem Bikes

Yes, the bicycle built for two is still around, and better than ever. Tandems are available in road, mountain, and hybrid versions. Tandems are great for mismatched riders as the stronger rider can never get too far ahead of the weaker rider! Tandems have heavy-duty wheels and advanced frame structures to support the weight of two riders. They often have disc brakes for additional stopping power.

Cargo Bikes

Cargo bikes may have extended seat and chain stays to allow for longer racks and platforms to be installed over the rear wheel, or they may have a cargo platform in front of the rider. Some versions are tricycles, like the old bicycle-powered ice cream cart. Cargo bikes have gearing and brakes to handle heavy load acceleration and deceleration.

Tandem bike

Cargo bike

CHAPTER 2

Get Riding!

You have your bike ready to roll, and now it's time to get out there.
It is important that you understand the basics of how your bike works.
The brakes may save your life and the gears will certainly save your
knees. It's also good to know that there are right ways and wrong
ways to sit on a bike, because how you
sit on the bike will affect your comfort
and your longevity as a biker.

There are many ways to improve your biking
skills and strength for your commute, daylong
rides, hill climbs, or bike tour. If you are riding
off-road for the first time, there are specific skills
to develop for this kind of biking.

Hydration and nutrition are discussed in
this chapter, and some hints about how to avoid
common bicycling aches and pains.

If you haven't been on your bike for a while,
or you have purchased a new bike, take the time
to practice. This will improve your skills and
awareness, and make you a safer rider. You may
feel silly riding around in circles in a parking lot,
but try to relax and enjoy building your skills.

Practicing in a controlled environment is the best way to build basic riding skills. Practice gear
shifting, braking, and maneuvering through obstacles.

BIKE RIDING SKILLS

Regardless of how much you have ridden, there are always ways to improve your riding skills. Time in the saddle is, of course, the primary way to do this. But some reminders on posture, shifting gears, braking, safety, and security are always helpful.

If it has been years since you have ridden a bike, it's a good idea to practice in a controlled environment before you hit the road or trail. A sidewalk or trail with soft grass on either side or an empty parking lot are both good places to start. Practice starting and stopping, riding in increasingly smaller circles and figure eights, and using your shifters to run through the gears. Use the brakes to stop suddenly and slowly and gently. Practice getting on and off the bike. Carefully practice standing up and pedaling.

Bicycling Posture

Most people, including some long-time cyclists, do not realize how important rider posture is. Poor posture puts excess strain on your body and makes it more difficult to enjoy longer rides. If you already have poor walking or sitting posture, chances are your cycling posture will also be poor.

- Regardless of bike style, always ride with your shoulders down and back, not up around your ears or rounded forward. You should not look like a vulture on your bike. Riding with your shoulders up and forward puts more strain on your neck, even when riding an upright, comfort bike.

- Your back should be flat, not arched like a hissing cat. Bend at the hips, not in an arc along the upper back. Riders of mountain bikes and hybrid bikes often make the mistake of rounding the shoulders forward and locking the elbows to extend forward, rather than bending at the hips.

  - Your elbows should always be slightly bent. Locking the elbows puts stress on the ligaments of the elbow joint and will eventually cause pain. In addition, locking the elbows limits your reaction time and prevents you from absorbing road shock.

    - Riding a bike does require a certain amount of core, upper back, and arm strength. Unfortunately, riding a bike does not develop these areas, so it is important to participate in strength training (weightlifting) and flexibility training (yoga or Pilates).

Proper posture is crucial to biking comfort. Keep your back straight and flat, shoulders down and back, and elbows bent.

Braking

Safely coming to a stop is important. If your bike has rim brakes, there is a brake lever for each wheel. The left hand brake is for the front wheel, and the right hand brake is for the rear wheel. Due to the physics of braking, the front brake is more powerful. Walk beside your bike and apply the front brakes suddenly. The bike will stop and the back wheel will lift off the ground. Walk beside the bike and apply the rear brakes suddenly. The rear tire will skid. This is because the momentum of the bike is to the front.

When braking with hand brakes, always use both brakes. Apply double or triple the amount of force to the front brake (left lever) compared to the rear brake. If you apply sudden, full force braking to the front wheel alone, and you are riding downhill or at great speed, you may flip the bike over the abruptly halted front wheel. Sudden braking to the rear wheel will lock up the wheel and cause it to skid. If your bike has a coaster brake, you engage the brake by applying backward pressure on the pedals. The brake works on the rear hub and brings the rear wheel to a stop.

Sudden braking can result in your body being thrown against the top tube or the handlebar stem. (Ouch!) Practicing various levels of braking in a controlled environment will make you familiar with these forces and better able to counteract the deceleration. While moving very slowly, practice braking hard enough with the front brake to lift the rear wheel. Practice braking with the rear brake hard enough to skid. Practice both actions together. Practice moving your weight toward the back of the bike to offset the forward momentum. If you feel like you are losing control of the bike, release the brakes. Wear your helmet!

Do not apply the brakes during a turn. This demands that you think ahead. Brake before entering a turn, or, if on a long sweeping downhill, brake lightly. Sharp braking on gravel or sand will result in a skid.

Braking in Wet Conditions

Wet conditions create a totally different braking environment, unless you have disc brakes. Rim brakes operate through friction between the brake pad and the rim. Wet or muddy rims and pads do not generate as much friction. In addition, your tires do not have as much grip on wet surfaces. Stopping distances under these conditions are increased substantially. Brake lightly on slippery surfaces to prevent the front wheel from skidding, and pump the brakes when wet to dry out the rims and pads.

The forward momentum of the bicycle causes the rear wheel to leave the ground when only the front brake is applied suddenly. Shifting the body weight toward the back of the bike and applying both brakes prevents this.

Wearing a Helmet

Make sure you are wearing your helmet properly. The helmet should fit your head snugly. It should sit level on your head, with the front an inch or less above your eyebrows. The strap should have no more than two fingers width of slack.

For further discussion of helmet selection and usage, see pages 48 to 49.

Starting from a Stop

How do you create momentum when starting from a stop? A bike is difficult to balance if you are moving too slowly, so it is important to build momentum quickly when starting from a stop. The best way to do this is to properly position your pedals for takeoff. Every rider has a foot he or she favors for placing on the ground first. With the other foot, rotate the pedal backwards so that it is nearly at the front top of its rotation. When you start pedaling, you will now have a full range of pedal thrust on that side while you bring your other foot from the ground to the pedal. Practice this maneuver so it becomes second nature, and you won't be wobbling across intersections while others are shooting past.

To initiate momentum from a complete stop, the rider stands over the stopped bike, leaning forward slightly. The near foot should be on a pedal that is positioned between noon and 1 o'clock. The far foot is on the ground.

Shifting Gears

If you have looked at other bicycling books, you may have been overwhelmed, or at least somewhat intimidated, by the lengthy discussions of gearing and inches and ratios. Don't worry: It is possible to enjoy riding your bike for decades without having the faintest understanding of any of this information. You should, however, have a working knowledge of how the shifter on your bike works and how to maximize your riding efficiency. As you become a more advanced rider, you can delve as deeply into the endless gearing debate as you care to.

The majority of bike shifting mechanisms require that you be actively pedaling to shift gears. This is because the derailleur moves in a manner that pushes, lifts, or drops the chain onto different sprockets. Without chain movement, the derailleur cannot perform these actions. Internal hub gears work slightly differently. You can move the shifter when the bike is stopped or when coasting. With either gearing system, however, it is important not to attempt to shift when excessive force is being applied to the chain.

Most bicycles are equipped with multiple chainrings (the toothed rings located by the pedals) and cassettes with multiple sprockets (the cluster of toothed rings on the rear wheel). Read more about these parts on pages 94 and 97 in the Bicycle Overview chapter. Some bikes are equipped with an internal gear hub. All the gearing is hidden inside the hub of the rear wheel.

On a bike that has three chainrings and eight or nine sprockets on the cassette, you would think that you had 24 or 27 speeds. Because of the crossover configuration of the chain between the chainrings and the cassette, two or three gears will not be usable. (Don't worry, 20 options is still plenty.)

When the chain is on the smallest chainring (front) and the smallest sprocket (rear), the derailleur typically cannot take up all the resulting chain slack, and the derailleur pulleys will ride up against the cassette. It is not particularly productive to ride in this gear. The opposite issue, with the chain on the largest chainring and largest sprocket, results in an angle that compromises chain strength. Therefore, these gearing combinations are not effective or useable.

Downshift before you get to a stop sign, especially if the road on the other side of the intersection goes uphill. Trying to get started in a high gear from a full stop can be difficult and dangerous.

29

TIP

Gear Numbers

A low bike gear with a corresponding low number is one that is easy to pedal. The ease in pedaling has a drawback, which is that the bike does not move as far per pedal rotation. A high bike gear number is harder to push, but yields greater travel distance. It is the same relationship as in automobiles with standard transmissions.

Bike Chain Positions

To make your riding as efficient as possible, it is important to become thoroughly familiar with your gear options. The best way to do this is find an empty parking lot or quiet street and practice. Wear your helmet! Begin by shifting into the lowest (easiest) gear. This is the smallest chainring on the front and the largest sprocket on the back. If the shifters have numeric labels, shift so that each shifter is on "1." On a bike with internal hub gears, shift to "1." Pedal around a bit and see how easy it is to pedal but how slowly you progress forward. Shift through the rear sprockets (right hand shifter) one at a time to feel how the pedaling resistance changes and how much farther you move on each pedal stroke.

You might notice that the left hand shifter activates the front derailleur, and the right hand shifter activates the rear derailleur. (And you may remember that the left hand brake lever activates the front brake and the right hand brake lever activates the rear brake.) You may also notice that the movement needed to go to easier gears on the left side is the movement used to go to harder gears on the right side. This is why you need to accustom yourself to the gears. With practice, you won't have to think about which way to shift to go up or down, and you won't have to take your eyes off the road to look at the numbers on your shifter or the position of the chain on the chainring and sprocket.

If you have a bike with triple front chainrings, do not use the smallest front chainring with the two or three smallest sprockets on the rear. Once you have shifted through the rear sprockets, shift back to the second or third largest rear sprocket, then shift to the larger front chainring. Progress through the rear gears again. Remember you are moving from larger (lower) gears in the rear to smaller (higher) gears. When you arrive at the smallest rear sprocket you will find that a great deal of effort is needed to push the pedals around, even on flat ground. (If you have a mountain bike, the gearing may be somewhat lower, so the highest gears won't be so tough.)

Once you have shifted through all the gears, try starting from a stop in the lowest (easiest, smallest in front, largest in rear) gear, in a middle gear, and in the highest (hardest, largest in front, smallest in back) gear. You'll feel quite a difference. Now imagine you are riding along with the wind at your back on a gently sloping downhill. You have shifted into your highest gear so you can still pedal without flying off the bike. Up ahead is a stop sign, and after the stop the road begins to go uphill. If you stop without shifting gears, you will be stuck in a situation where it becomes difficult to shift. That is because the derailleur system requires that you be pedaling to shift, but also is limited in that you cannot apply full cranking force to the chain while shifting. In this instance, you want to shift before you come to a stop. In fact, it is best to determine what your favorite start up gear is, and always shift into that when stopping.

Riding in hilly terrain will give you the ultimate practice for efficient shifting. If you wait too long when climbing a hill to shift into easier gears, it becomes difficult to shift. The front derailleur can usually drop the chain from the large chainring to the smaller, but the rear derailleur is pushing the chain up onto the larger rear sprockets and it cannot do this when the pressure on the chain is too great.

The bike is in the lowest (easiest) gear when the chain is on the smallest chainring in front and the largest sprocket in back.

The bike is in the highest (hardest) gear when the chain is on the largest chainring in front and the smallest sprocket in back.

Cross chaining happens when the chain is on the largest chainring and largest sprocket or when the chain is on the smallest chainring and smallest sprocket. Cross chaining damages the chain, and is usually noisy.

When the chain is on the smallest chainring and the smallest sprocket, the derailleur rides very close to the sprockets and the loose chain slaps around.

Spin, Spin, Spin

Want to bike all day without hurting your knees? Many cyclists make the mistake of pedaling in a high gear (hard to pedal) then pausing and coasting, pedaling and coasting, pedaling and coasting. This manner of riding is actually inefficient and hard on your leg muscles and knees. It is much easier on your body to pedal constantly in an easy gear.

When biking on a bike with multiple gears, you can practice riding with different cadences, or pedaling tempos. By putting your bike in a lower gear (easier to pedal) you can spin, which means you are pedaling at a high cadence. If you desire to get technical, you can purchase a cycle computer that includes a cadence sensor. The cadence sensor tells you how many pedal revolutions per minute you are doing. Aim for a 60-rpm cadence to begin with. This is easy to figure, because you should be able to count one Mississippi for each full rotation one of your feet makes with the pedal. Try to maintain this consistently on flat ground and gentle hills.

The purpose of spinning is to build endurance and create a smoother pedaling technique. Your muscle output per pedal revolution in low gear is very small; ideally, it should feel like you are exerting only a small amount of force.

Once you have gotten into the habit of consistently pedaling at about 60 rpm, work on increasing your cadence. Practice on a flat stretch of road and shift into an

A cadence sensor accurately counts pedal revolutions.

uncomfortably easy (low) gear and pedal as fast as you can. Initially you will feel foolish and your body will seem to be flopping all over the place as you move your legs so quickly. The more you practice, the smoother your pedal stroke will become. Attempt to push your pedal rpms over 100. This will be uncomfortable at first, but eventually you will become accustomed to it.

Timing your cadence without a sensor is difficult, but you really don't need the number. Simply push yourself to move your feet as fast as you can and still be comfortable and in control of the bike. Note: Spinning very fast should only be done if you have toe clips or clipless pedals and shoes. When your feet are moving so quickly it is very easy to slip off the pedals. Slipping off the pedals is a major cause of bike accidents.

In daily riding, always choose the lowest gear (easiest) that you can comfortably ride in without feeling like you might fly off the bike from pedaling so quickly. You will be able to ride farther and feel less fatigue by riding in this way, as opposed to riding in the highest (hardest) gear to pedal in.

The drawback of spinning is that you do not have the potential for quick acceleration. Because you are in a low gear, you move the pedals around a lot for a small amount of forward movement. In order to accelerate quickly, you must use a higher gear where each pedal revolution pushes the bike farther. Using higher gears requires more power.

For routine road cycling, try to maintain a consistent cadence in the neighborhood of 60 pedal revolutions per minute. If your cadence exceeds this rate significantly, you should wear toe clips to prevent slippage.

Professional cyclists ride at high cadences in high gears to attain steady speeds of twenty-five to thirty miles an hour.

The only way to get faster and stronger is to build power by interval training and hill climbing.

Building Power

Like most riders, as you gain experience on your bike you'll want to see improvement in your cycling power and speed. In order to go faster, you have to increase your leg strength and your aerobic capacity. This alone will allow you to comfortably spin in higher and harder gears. Your pedal cadence multiplied by a higher gear will move you farther and faster.

You can begin to focus on building power after you have been riding consistently for a few weeks. It is important to take care of your knees, and pushing hard gears before your legs are accustomed to cycling will be painful or potentially injurious. To build power, find a long flat stretch of road or trail to practice on. Get up to your normal speed with a quick cadence. Shift into the hardest gear you can pedal in and ride for a hundred yards—you should be breathing hard at the end. After a hundred yards, shift back into your regular gear for another hundred yards or until your breathing returns to normal. Repeat this until you can no longer pedal in the high gear. Make certain to stretch your hamstrings and quadriceps after this exercise. Do this exercise a couple times per week. You will soon see its impact on your regular riding, as you will be able to more easily maintain your cadence in higher and higher gears.

You can also build strength on the bike by riding hills. Instead of shifting down to your lowest gear, try increasing the gear that you use to ride a hill. When you get to the top, ride back down, spinning as you go, and repeat. If you live in an area that is pancake flat where highway overpasses are the only hills, you may need to do this strength training off the bike with lower-body weightlifting moves such as lunges and squats.

Pacing

Pacing is all about adapting your riding style to the length and difficulty of a particular ride. The goal is to end your ride physically tired, but not utterly exhausted. If you are riding a 150-mile weekend tour, burning yourself out by riding at the top level of your fitness on the first day won't be enjoyable. Decrease your cadence for rides that are longer than your average ride, or more difficult due to wind or hills. If you wear your work clothes to commute, it's usually a good idea to pace yourself to minimize sweating.

Riding Hills

Some cyclists hate hills and some love hills. Hills can be short and steep, rolling, or long and gradual. When climbing steep or long hills you won't be able to maintain your cadence. Shift into a comfortable, low gear and work your way up the hill at whatever cadence gets you to the top without shooting your heart rate into the stratosphere. Lean your body weight forward as much as possible. Keep your upper body relaxed and try not to pull on the handlebars as you pedal—this expends energy that is needed by your legs.

At times you may need or want to stand up to either push past a very steep grade or provide some variety in your pedaling. If you are riding with drop bars, position your hands on the drops or over the brake hoods. If you are riding a mountain bike with bar ends, either position works well.

On downhill runs, brake before you need to, and overestimate how slowly you need to go through turns. You will be surprised how quickly your momentum builds as you zip downhill. On straight roads, you may want to go faster—an aero tuck will give you more speed.

Standing is an excellent way to cope with short steep inclines, or to give yourself a break from sitting. Lean forward slightly to maintain your balance.

Decrease your wind resistance when coasting downhill by getting into an aerodynamic tuck. Remember to look ahead and keep your hands near the brakes.

Off-Road Riding

Riding off-road requires some special techniques beyond the basic riding skills needed for pavement. Off-road trails have steeper ascents and descents. Trail riding, whether it is on single-track (wide enough for one bike), fire or logging roads (wider, but still dirt), or gravel surfaces, leads to encounters with tree roots, logs, rocks, loose gravel, potholes, and sand. One fact that quickly becomes obvious as you embark on off-road biking is that you spend a lot less time sitting down and a lot more time as a human shock absorber.

Maintaining a consistent cadence while off-road riding is not possible. Due to trail conditions, you will often need to pedal very hard, then coast with the pedals at 9 and 3 o'clock positions to clear rocks and roots.

The most important skills for off-road riding are the ability to move your body to change how the bike is weighted, and developing good upper body strength and balance. Sometimes the rider's weight needs to be way back over the rear wheel, and sometimes it needs to be over the front wheel. Side to side control is also important to keep the bike steady over uneven terrain. A mountain biking clinic or some one-on-one instruction from a friend who bikes off road is a great way to learn the skills needed for this sport.

When riding off-road, it's no fun (and inefficient) to dismount and pick the bike up over logs or rocks. The point of the mountain bike configuration is that it can be used to ride or jump over many obstacles. If you have a mountain bike and plan to do some trail riding, take the time to practice these skills in a controlled environment. Fortunately, with the mountain bike's big squishy tires, practicing on nice soft grass is easy. Make sure

Wheelies aren't just stunts for kids on their Sting Rays. Developing the skills to wheelie and bunny hop is important for off-road riding.

Practice shifting your weight all the way to the back of the bike, even behind the seat.

Practice shifting your weight so it is over the handlebars.

that you have practiced all of the basic riding skills and are comfortable with the bike. And always wear your helmet and gloves.

Begin to develop your off-road skills by working on your weight shift movements. While the bike is rolling, stand on the pedals with the pedals parallel to the ground (3 o'clock and 9 o'clock position). Move your rear end all the way back past the back of the seat, while keeping your knees and elbows bent. Adjust your bike seat downward if it feels like it is in the way—mountain bikes have quick release levers on the seat. Then, practice moving your weight forward over the handlebars—keeping the pedals parallel to the ground and your knees and elbows bent.

Next, practice moving your weight up and down. This is how to create the springing force that will move the bike over obstacles. In the same riding position, quickly bend your elbows and move your body downward. Then, without hesitation, push your body upwards and pull up on the handlebars. This will lift the front wheel off the ground. Practice doing this without an obstacle; then practice this move to go up over a curb. Make sure to approach perpendicular to the curb. As soon as the front wheel is over the curb, move your body weight forward and pull your feet up toward your chest. This will move the weight to the front of the bike and the rear wheel will roll over the curb. As you get better and better at moving your weight and creating spring, you will be able to bunny hop the bike over obstacles.

Also practice going down off the curb. Standing, with the pedals parallel to the ground, knees and elbows bent and weight toward the rear, roll off the curb. Use your arms and legs to absorb the shock.

Off-Road and Inclines

Climbing and descending on rough trails also requires special skills. Off-road riding requires even more gear shifting skill than riding on paved roads. Going uphill and shifting into a super low gear and spinning on loose soil or sand will only result in the rear wheel spinning and the bike stalling out. Keep your weight slightly forward while climbing—even so, sometimes the front wheel will come off the ground.

On a descent, shift your rear end behind the seat, and hold the seat between your thighs. Keep your knees and elbows bent and relaxed. Your index and middle fingers should be on the brake levers at all times. It is important to brake carefully. Too much braking on the rear wheel will cause skidding, which diminishes control and ruins the trail. Too much braking on the front wheel increases the possibility of flying over the handlebars. Make sure you focus on the path you want to take, not the obstacles you want to avoid. If you stare at the big rock poking up in the trail, you will hit it!

Lean forward when riding up hill to keep the front wheel in contact with the ground. Stand up to gain leverage and generate more power.

To maintain control while riding downhill, shift your weight behind the seat and keep your knees and elbows bent.

Off-Road Rules

Off-road riding can be destructive and dangerous if basic principles are not followed. Mountain bikes, with their knobby tires, can quickly destroy trails and wildlife. Hikers and cyclists also tend to share trails, which can lead to dangerous encounters. Consequently, the International Mountain Bicycling Association (IMBA) has developed a list of rules for off-road riding. Along with abiding by basic safety practices, you should follow these rules at all times.

- Ride at appropriate speeds to prevent harsh braking and skidding.
- Wet or muddy trails are quickly degraded when ridden on—choose another day to ride if your favorite dirt trail is wet.
- If you encounter a puddle on the trail, go through it—do not widen the path by going around obstacles. You are on a mountain bike, after all.
- Be especially considerate of hikers and horseback riders. Bombing down a trail when you can't see around the bend can have catastrophic results. Some off-road riders treat other trail users inconsiderately. This type of conflict results in limited access for all off-road users.
- Ride on open trails only—do not trespass on private land, do not ride on trails marked "No Biking," do not ride in federally protected wilderness areas.
- Leave no trace—don't ride on muddy or wet trails, do not create new trails or ride off the trail to avoid obstacles. Pack out all trash—no exceptions.
- Control your bicycle—ride within your limits.
- Yield to others—bicycles must yield to all other trail users (horses and pedestrians) unless the trail is marked bicycles only.
- Never scare animals
- Plan ahead—go equipped with the proper gear for terrain, weather, and emergencies.

Observe and obey all usage signs that pertain to cyclists of any type.

Bicyclists must use care when sharing a trail with other users.

The sun and wind work quickly to dehydrate cyclists. Learning how to take a drink while riding is an important skill to master, since it won't be a fun ride if you have to stop to take a sip.

Hydration and Nutrition

It is common for beginning cyclists who are increasing their ride duration or intensity to misjudge how much water or food they need. Cycling is a fairly dehydrating activity, and riding at a moderate or high intensity burns between 500 to 600 calories per hour.

A cyclist creates his or her own breeze that causes sweat to evaporate rapidly. As you are riding, you don't realize how much fluid you are losing. It is important to have water with you if you are riding for more than twenty minutes. While riding at moderate to high intensity, you should drink four to eight ounces of water every 15 or 20 minutes. The easiest way to do this is to drink one bike bottle of water per hour. If it is very hot or very humid, eating a banana or drinking an electrolyte drink will help prevent cramping.

When cycling for longer than two hours at a time, you will also need to replenish your body's glycogen levels. Cyclists use the term "bonk" to refer to the light-headedness, shakiness, and fatigue that happens from depleting ones glycogen stores. You need not be an endurance cyclist to experience this—in fact, it happens to cyclists at any level who have ridden a bit too long without food. What's interesting is that you may not realize it while on the bike and riding. Often you experience it when you stop and you keel over without warning. Besides being embarrassing, this is potentially quite dangerous. When your glycogen levels are depleted, your brain processing speed slows down. It is very easy to make serious errors in judgment when your glycogen is low.

Even if you are carrying a little extra weight, your body cannot convert stored fat into fuel quickly enough to keep up with your rate of consumption. The moral of the story is, make sure to bring along something to eat if you will be riding at moderate or high intensity for more than two hours. And don't wait until you feel hungry.

Stop, take a break and eat some energy food at regular intervals as you enjoy your cycling workout. Bananas are a prime, all-natural energy food.

The best food options are fruits like apples, oranges, and bananas. They contain nutrients and water, plus the sugar you need to keep going. Avoid candy bars and soda unless they are the only choice. They both contain too much simple sugar, which hits the bloodstream quickly and results in a blood sugar spike, and then a blood sugar crash about 20 or 30 minutes later. Energy bars and sports drinks work, but be aware that their high calorie counts might be more than you need or want.

Aches and Pains

Bicycle riding can be a pain in the butt. Literally. Also a pain in the neck, hands, and back. Some cycling pain is caused by the fit of the bike. A bike that is too long and causes the rider to stretch out will cause back and shoulder pain. A seat that is too high is likely to cause low back pain because the pelvis is rocking back and forth as the rider reaches for the bottom of every pedal stroke. A seat that is too low can cause knee pain.

Other pain can be caused by poor posture—even on a good fitting bike. Hyperextending or locking the elbows strains the elbow ligaments and decreases the shock absorption of the joint. Usually locking the elbows also results in the shoulders being shoved up around the ears. Elevated shoulders puts excess stress on the upper back muscles and strains the neck.

Don't ride like this. Riding with poor posture can be very painful and decreases the rider's flexibility to absorb impacts or make sudden maneuvers.

Riding with the palms facing inward and the wrists straight reduces stress on your wrists and your forearm tendons.

Hand and Wrist Pain

Hand and wrist pain is a common complaint of bicyclists. Riding with padded gloves and padded handlebars helps. More important, however, is to maintain the wrists in a straight line, not allowing the wrists to drop down to form a right angle at the joint. Think of how your wrists are aligned when your arms are relaxed at your sides. Maintain this straight line when riding. When the wrists are bent, stress is placed on the tendons that run through the wrist; this aggravates the tendons, which, when added to the pressure of the handlebar on the lower palm, can lead to carpal tunnel irritation. Unfortunately, the alignment of the brake levers on most hybrid and mountain bikes promotes a bent wrist riding posture. Have the bike shop loosen the levers and rotate them downward so you can ride with straight wrists and still have proper access to the brake levers.

Also, riding with the hands on a bar that is perpendicular to the body is the most uncomfortable for the wrist and forearms. Better to have a riding position where the hands are rotated so that the palms are facing inward rather than downward. Drop handlebars have numerous options for this position. Adding bar ends to flat mountain bike bars will allow for this position. Moving the hands around to different positions on the handlebars is important to prevent one area of the hand from becoming over used. If you don't have strong abdominal muscles, you may be riding with too much of your body weight on your hands.

If you have arthritis in the hands or wrists, or previous shoulder or elbow injuries, it is particularly important to ride with proper riding posture. You may also want to consider riding a suspension style bike to minimize the shock transfer. Steel and carbon fiber frames have more give and transfer less shock than aluminum frames. Riding in a more upright position will remove some weight from the hands. Some riders find no comfortable way to ride an upright bike, and find relief in riding a recumbent cycle.

Knee Pain

Knee pain is usually caused by a seat that is too low or by riding in a gear that is too high for your leg strength or the riding conditions. Raise your seat a quarter to one half inch and see if that helps. Also, use lower gears. When riding on a level grade, it should feel like you are exerting only minimal force (see pages 32 to 33).

Seat Pain

There is no way to totally prevent saddle soreness if you are biking for more than an hour at time. However, wearing bicycling shorts and choosing the proper seat for the type of riding you are doing will help in minimizing this pain. Upright riders need ample seat padding due to the increased proportion of weight being placed on the rear end. Wide padded seats are great for this type of riding. Riders who ride in a more extended posture need to use narrower seats to prevent chafing of the inner thighs and rear.

Your sit bones will be sore after your first long ride. They will be even sorer the next day if you get on a bike. The only remedy for this is to ride more often. Your body needs to become accustomed to the pressure points of the saddle. If you are still terrifically sore after a solid couple of weeks or so of riding, it is time to look at a different saddle.

If you are experiencing tailbone pain when riding, look for a seat with a groove or cut-out between the padded sides. This will provide a gap for your tailbone.

If you are experiencing chafing and are not wearing bicycling shorts, it's time to make the investment in proper shorts. Street clothes have numerous seams in all the wrong places for biking comfort. If you have chafing and you are wearing bike shorts, try anti-chafing cream. Most bike shops sell these creams in handy roll-on applicators. Make sure your shorts fit snugly enough that they are not riding up. And remember, no underwear with bike shorts.

Finally, it is important that you don't lounge around in your sweaty bike shorts after a long, hot ride. Change immediately into dry clothing. Always wash your shorts between rides. This is especially important if you are bike touring. Rashes and yeast infections have put an end to many a bike tourist's riding pleasure.

Neck Pain

Riding a road bike in the down position will place strain on the neck, especially if your riding posture is poor. When riding in a down position, make sure that your back is flat, your shoulders are back and down, and you are holding yourself in a relaxed way. Many road bikes are configured with the handlebars one to six inches below the level of the seat. Most casual riders or tourists do not need to ride in this extreme posture. Unless you are racing, make the handlebars level with the seat. Raising the handlebars will decrease neck pain.

Bicycle riding requires holding your upper body fairly still for long lengths of time. Counteract this stress by building up your strength through resistance (strength) training. Build flexibility by stretching, or practicing yoga or Pilates. These activities will increase your riding pleasure by decreasing the strain on your neck, back, and arms.

What if You Hurt All Over?

Many new riders complain of overall pain. This is often due to oxygen deprivation that results from insufficient blood flow. There are two ways you can address this: move your arms and back more while riding; do shoulder shrugs and rolls, arm windmills, and back stretches while on the bike; and stop frequently to do more shrugs and stretches. It's also important to build up these muscles with weight lifting and other exercises when off the bike.

CHAPTER 3

Safety and Security

There are numerous ways to hurt yourself while cycling, but it is also possible to ride for years and never have an accident or mishap. Most of us have been walking and running for decades, but we still occasionally slip or fall down. The same will be true of cycling. Practice your skills, wear a helmet, maintain your bike, follow the rules of the road, and choose appropriate bike routes to minimize your risks.

It is true that many cyclists are killed every year. It is also true that many pedestrians and motorists are killed every year. It is risky to leave the house, but it is also risky to sit on the couch and watch television.

Many bicyclists complain that motorists are particularly inattentive or rude to cyclists. It is important to remember two things. The first is to think of how many inattentive or rude drivers you encounter when driving your car or walking. The number of these types of drivers doesn't increase the instant you hop on your bike. Also, think of all the times you have seen cyclists behaving in rude or inattentive ways. The bottom line is, when you are on your bicycle, you are more vulnerable to motorists, pedestrians, and road hazards. That means you must be more careful, more consistent, and more aware while on your bicycle. The good news is, while you are on your bike, you are probably having more fun than motorists and pedestrians.

Pre-ride Bike Check

Before every ride:

- Squeeze the tires or use a pressure gauge to check tire pressure and inflate if necessary.

- Squeeze both brake levers and make sure the brake pads are making good contact with the rims. The levers should not make contact with the handlebars. The brake pads should not remain in contact with the rims after the levers are released.

- Check that the quick-release skewers on both wheels and the seat post (if present) are fully tightened.

Safety

Your safety on a bike depends on many factors. You can't stop that motorist from texting, but you can make sure your brakes work well. You also can diminish your risks by being smart about where, when, and how you choose to ride. Mentally preparing yourself for the challenges of riding in difficult situations will help you become a better, more attentive rider.

Inspect Your Bike Before Each Ride

Before each ride, always check that the brakes are working well, that the wheels' quick release levers are tight, that the seat post is tight, and that no clothing straps or shoelaces are near wheels, chain, or derailleurs. Shoelaces or pant legs caught in between the front chainring, chain, and derailleur can cause a crash. Detangling shoelaces from the front chainrings can be extremely difficult and certainly gets you very dirty. Straps that dangle from bags or panniers also can become lodged between the wheel and the bike frame, causing the bike to suddenly stop. A jacket or sweatshirt tied around the waist can get caught between the wheel and frame.

SAFETY TIP: To keep pant legs from getting caught in the front chainring, use a trouser clip or band to hold the fabric tight to your leg and away from the chainring. Many bands come with reflective striping for added safety protection.

Practice Your Skills

If you are comfortable on your bike and competent in your essential riding skills, you will be able to react quickly and safely to surprises or hazards. The opposite is also true: uncomfortable and inexperienced or inattentive riders are more likely to have accidents.

The most basic cycling skill to perfect is riding in a straight line. A wobbly, uncertain rider will be at risk of being hit by a car while on the street, or by other cyclists while on a trail. If you have difficulty controlling your bike and riding in a smooth straight line, you may need a better fitting (or just better) bike. Practice riding in a controlled area until you can comfortably maintain straight, forward motion. Also practice looking over your shoulders while maintaining the straight-line path. Because the bicycle is easily guided by body movement, when you look over your shoulder the bicycle tends to follow your eyes and veer in that direction if you are not careful.

In an empty parking lot, practice riding in circles and figure-eights. Practice applying the brakes and using the gear shifters while looking straight ahead. Practice signaling. Practice taking a drink of water while maintaining a straight line.

Twist, Tuck, and Roll

If you are riding wearing lace-up shoes, twist the loops and ends together and tuck this bundle under the lacing. This will prevent the laces from being caught up in the chain. If you are riding with long, loose pants, roll the right pant leg up above the level of the biggest chainring. Or, use a clip or strap to secure the leg so it doesn't get caught or dirtied by the chain.

Practice all of the basic cycling maneuvers in a safe area. This includes taking the water bottle from the cage, taking a drink, and replacing the bottle while riding in a straight line with eyes forward.

Approvals

Bicycle helmets must be approved by the Consumer Product Safety Commission. Do not buy a helmet that doesn't have this approval. For a higher level of safety, you may be able to find helmets approved by the Snell Foundation. New designs are rigorously tested to assure they meet the basic standards set by these organizations.

Wear a Helmet

Wearing a helmet while cycling is the single most important safety measure you can take. You will recover from a skinned palm or a broken wrist or rib, but a severe concussion or traumatic brain injury can change your life forever.

Most bike accidents involve a blow to the head. The forward momentum of your body suddenly stopped by impact with the ground or other fixed object will whip your head with increased force into that object. Watch a few slow motion clips on the Internet of bike accidents and you will see riders' heads smashing into the ground.

The bike helmet is engineered to do two things: prevent laceration and absorb impact. The hard shell on the outside of the helmet is meant to allow the helmet to slide over the impact surface and also to prevent the head from being cut. The dense foam of the helmet provides a crush zone to decrease the impact speed. The typical bike helmet is meant to be destroyed in a crash, so if you do crash with this type of helmet, you must replace it. Hard-shell BMX helmets are meant to provide protection for repeated falls, as might happen if you are learning to ride or performing tricks.

Bicycle helmets are designed to balance consumer desire for ventilation and light weight against safety features. The resulting helmets do not provide maximum protection (that would be a motorcycle helmet), but they do provide a level of protection far greater than riding bareheaded.

Wearing a helmet is not a perfect guarantee against brain injury, but helmet use can prevent a minor accident from turning into a lifelong headache or death. According to many statistics, 95 to 97 percent of cyclists who died in crashes were not wearing helmets.

Bicycle helmets come in two popular styles: the common vented helmet (left) and the BMX style (right).

Many cyclists make the mistake of thinking that if they ride on a dedicated bike trail they don't need to wear a helmet because there is no vehicle traffic. And some may even go so far as to think sticking to the marked bicycle lanes in street traffic somehow insulates them from mishaps. Although keeping to bike trails and lanes is safer than riding in open traffic, dangers beyond your control always exist, making the wearing of a helmet a mandatory practice and a good habit to boot. Bike trails have a high volume of novice users, non-cyclists, dog walkers, and other random hazards. You will hit the ground just as hard whether on the street or a bike trail.

Make sure you wear your helmet correctly. It should fit your head snugly with the front of the helmet no more than one inch above your eyebrows; it certainly shouldn't be perched atop your head. The straps should be snug—no more than two finger widths of slack under the chin.

Don't ride like this. Many people mistakenly think that helmets are just for kids, or that they are not as necessary if you stick to trails or bike lanes.

In proper adjustment, your helmet should be flat on your head and snug. The front of the helmet should be parallel with, and no more than 1″ above, your eyebrows. The bottom of the V on each side of the strap should fall just under the ears, and when buckled the strap should be snug but not uncomfortable, with no more than two fingers-width of slack.

Do's and Don'ts

Don't Ride Against Traffic

Riding against traffic is very unsafe: in fact, it is illegal in every state in the U.S. There are many reasons for this. First, bicycles are considered vehicles and are expected to follow the same rules of the road as motorcycles, cars, and trucks. Pedestrians are not vehicles, which is why pedestrians walk against traffic when there is no sidewalk.

If you ride against traffic, you increase the likelihood that vehicle drivers and pedestrians will not see you because you are in the wrong lane. No one expects you there, so it is likely you will be hit, or at least sworn at.

Another reason not to ride against traffic is the combined speed factor. If you are riding with traffic at 15 mph and a car overtakes you at 30 mph, the driver is approaching you at 15 mph. The driver sees you ahead and has time to evaluate the situation and oncoming vehicles, and anticipate whether to slow down and wait to pass, or simply to pass. If you are riding headfirst into traffic at the same speeds, you and the car are now approaching each other at 45 mph (your 15 mph plus their 30 mph). Even if they come to a dead stop, you are still coming at them at 15 mph. If they swerve to go around you, they are running into oncoming traffic that they have not had the time to evaluate.

Finally, riding against traffic puts you in a hazardous position at intersections. If a car going the same direction as you is turning left and you are proceeding in a straight line, not only is it unlikely that you will see their turn signal, but it is likely that they will hit you. A motorist turning right onto the road that a wrong-way cyclist is traveling will not see the cyclist—the motorist is looking into oncoming traffic lanes, not the lane into which they are turning.

Even though there are wide variations in reporting of bicycle accidents and fatalities, there is high agreement across studies that riding on the wrong side of the road increases the accident and fatality risk by 4 to 7 times. Even riding on the sidewalk on the wrong side of the road increases your risk of being hit by a motorist.

Don't Ride on Sidewalks

Although it is counterintuitive, riding on sidewalks is more dangerous than riding on the street in the direction of traffic. Why? Sidewalks are designed for pedestrians who can stop instantaneously. When a car shoots out of a driveway or an alley obscured by shrubbery, the pedestrian usually hears the car coming and stops, or sees the car and leaps back in time. A cyclist traveling down the sidewalk at 10 mph (a very average cycling speed) will hit the car before seeing it.

Don't ride like this. Never ride your bike against traffic (and always wear a helmet). If you are sensitive to pollution or allergens a particle mask is recommended.

Don't Listen to Music While You Cycle

Most of us love to listen to music. But wearing headphones and listening to music while cycling is a bad idea. You can't hear vehicles as they approach you from the rear or side. You also can't hear your bike. If you could hear the ticking of your untied shoelace against the chainrings, you could stop and tie your shoe before getting caught up and thrown off balance.

Do Signal Your Turn

A key factor to safe cycling is being predictable. Signaling your intentions allows those around you to know where you will be next. You can use the standard hand signals taught to drivers—left turn, left arm pointed straight to the left; right turn, left arm out and bent up at 90 degrees; stop, left arm out and bend down at 90 degrees. Because cyclists are able to use both arms to signal, it is common for a right turn to be signaled by a right outstretched arm. Because many people are now unfamiliar with hand signals, pointing in the direction of your turn is more clear. Don't be lazy—fully extend your arm so your intentions are clear.

Hand Signals

LEFT: Fully extend your arm straight to the left.

RIGHT: Fully extend your arm straight to the right to signal a right turn.

STOP: Bend your left arm at a 90-degree angle pointing downward to signal a stop.

Road Hazards

Bicycles are more affected by road conditions than cars. Cars may bang through potholes or pass over sand without much ado, but bicycles can be aversely affected by many seemingly insignificant road features.

Railroad tracks are hazardous to cyclists, as this sign in Portland, Oregon, points out.

Rumble Strips

Rumble strips are pressed or machined bumps installed on shoulders of highways. Meant to wake sleepy drivers if they drift off the road, rumble strips are dangerous for cyclists. Most state transportation departments have stopped installing strips on roads potentially used for cycling, and cycling groups are lobbying every state to follow suit.

Cracks

Cracks in the road surface can make even the most practiced cyclist take a fall. Be very mindful of cracks running parallel to the curb. Cracks that are roughly the same width as a bike tire can cause you to lose control of the bike as you try and get out of the crack. If you find yourself riding in a crack, come to a stop, lift the bike out of the crack and proceed. It is difficult to make a controlled exit from this type of hazard.

Potholes

Hitting a pothole can flatten a tire or bend a rim; swerving to avoid a pothole can put you into the line of traffic or parked cars. Sometimes it is necessary to hit a pothole. If this is the case, brake as much as possible, stand on the pedals with the pedals parallel to the ground, and bend your elbows. The goal is to absorb as much of the shock of the pothole as possible.

Buckling

Pavement, whether asphalt or cement, can buckle or become wavy. Hitting these waves or buckles at high speed will jolt you and possibly buck you off the bike. If you are riding without toe clips or clipped pedals, your feet may slip from the pedals and cause you to fall off the seat. Slow down if you see you are approaching buckles or waves.

Water

Wet pavement can be extremely slick. When riding on wet pavement, slow down and ride as upright as possible. Do not lean into corners. Water on metal and paint creates a zero traction situation, so take care not to hit access covers or road striping in the arc of your turn.

Railroad Tracks

Railroad tracks crossing your path at a diagonal are very hazardous. Even on the smoothest crossings there are grooves between the pavement and the tracks. These grooves will catch your tires and toss you in an instant. The best way to cross tracks is to orient your bike so you are perpendicular to the tracks. This is critical if the tracks are wet. Before adjusting for the perpendicular crossing, make sure this maneuver doesn't put you in the line of traffic.

Sand and Gravel

Sand or loose gravel in the roadway is very dangerous. If you are riding a bike with skinny tires and you hit deep sand or gravel (like on the road shoulder) you will instantly lose speed and control. If you hit sand or gravel on the roadway while turning, it can cause you to lose control and fall on the turn.

Night Riding

There are many dangers inherent in riding a bike at night. Almost all of them have to do with visibility. In darkness you are limited in what you can see, and other cyclists and motorists can't see you. Lights and reflectors are critical night riding equipment that is required in most cities.

Even if you ride on a dead smooth, straight-as-an-arrow asphalt bike path, hazards spring up. If you have no light to illuminate your path, you might not see the garbage bag full of trash that a raccoon has strewn about the trail. Hitting the trash, not to mention the raccoon, at full speed is likely to cause a tumble. Therefore, you need some kind of light to shine on the path in front of you.

Headlamps and handlebar lamps come in an awe-inspiring variety. Before you plunk down $500 for a bike light (yes, you can pay that much), think about what type of riding you will be doing at night, and how dark night is where you ride. The $500 headlamp is for riders who ride 24-hour races in rural areas where there is little ambient light. For the urban commuter, a $25 light might do perfectly well to illuminate the pavement in between streetlights.

LED (light emitting diode) technology has done much to increase the brightness and the battery life of cycling headlights. The LED, in combination with advanced lens systems, can create a blindingly bright light.

If you ride regularly at dusk or night, consider getting a rechargeable lighting system, or at least using rechargeable batteries in a standard system. Most headlights come with three settings: high, low, and flash. Battery life for the high settings might run from three to ten hours, depending on the system. Battery life for the flash setting is usually three to ten times the steady run time.

As with daytime riding, nighttime riders are least visible to oncoming and crossing vehicles. To increase your chances of being seen, use flashing lights. Reflectors on wheels show up very well in car headlights, but only if the bike is perpendicular to the car. A flashing red taillight is required for night riding in some urban areas. The battery life for the flashing taillight seems indefinite—in the range of 100 to 300 hours. Reflective clothing is also a good idea. Vests and jackets are available with reflective striping or made entirely of reflective fabric.

LED bicycle safety lights have much longer battery life than older bike lights. Use them in combination with reflectors.

Reflective clothing specially designed for cycling greatly increases your visibility and makes nighttime riding a much safer pursuit..

Animal Hazards

Dogs can be a major threat to your safety, especially in rural areas where it is common for them to be unleashed. Fortunately, you can often out ride a dog. Unfortunately, you will often become closely acquainted with a dog while slowly slogging up a long hill. Before the dog reaches you, firmly shout, "No!" If this simple measure does not work, and the dog is gaining ground, prepare to give it a squirt of water from your water bottle; aim for the face. This usually gives you enough time to move past their range. Do not kick the dog. Not only does this slow you down, and speed is your prime defense against a dog, but it also moves the dog into a more aggressive state.

Most dogs will simply run and bark along the edge of the road without nipping at you. Once you exit their established territory, they usually back off. Occasionally, however, dogs succeed in taking a chunk of skin from a heel or calf. In really bad situations, you may need to dismount and retreat, holding the bike between you and the dog.

Squirrels can be an urban riding challenge. They seem to have a perpetual dare amongst themselves about who can dart into the street the most times without getting killed. The best thing to do is maintain your steady pace and direction; they typically move. Slow down, shout or ring your bell if they seem to be content sitting in your line of travel.

In rural areas, if you are off-road or road riding, it is probable that you will encounter wildlife or farm animals, especially at dusk or dawn. The most likely scenario for a crash is during a rapid descent. Most animals freeze briefly when startled, and if you are hurtling along at 30 mph on a big downhill, this moment is enough to keep them in your line. The best option is to be overly cautious descending during these times.

Dogs think chasing cyclists is great fun. Even if they don't want to bite you, they can get tangled in your wheels or pedals.

You never know who (or what) you'll meet on a bike trail.

Riding In Traffic

Riding in traffic is an intimidating proposition. If you are a novice biker, you should plan your routes to avoid heavily trafficked areas. If you must ride in heavy traffic without benefit of marked bike lanes, here are some pointers.

The most common car-bike accidents involve oncoming or turning cars. Cars overtaking you are most likely to see you. Drivers coming toward you are looking at the cars coming at them; they may not see you against the background of moving and parked cars. A large number of bike-car accidents involve drivers making left hand turns. They have waited for an opening in traffic and they see one, but they don't see you. Always assume that a left turning oncoming car has not seen you.

Generally when riding on multi-lane urban streets, you want to ride out from the curb or parked cars at least three feet. This positioning gives you plenty of leeway to avoid road hazards like potholes and also puts you far enough out into the lane that you are visible to cars and don't blend into the background. If you are riding alongside a row of parked cars, three feet is enough clearance to avoid the suddenly opened car door.

If you are able to ride the same speed as the traffic is flowing, you can take your place in the lane as if you were a car. If you are not moving as fast as traffic, you should position yourself so that traffic can flow around you. Even though you may have the right to be on the road, it does not pay to aggravate drivers by taking up a whole lane if you are moving slowly. Again, if you can't consistently ride at traffic speeds, you probably should be looking for a different route.

On a street without parked cars, you may want to ride closer to the curb to allow traffic to pass. This is dependent upon the condition of the curb area and the prevalence of storm grates.

TIP

Don't Swoop
When riding on a busy road with a parking lane, some riders swoop closer to the curb in the gaps where no cars are parked. You are more visible to drivers if you maintain a straight line a fixed distance from the curb.

Don't ride like this. Cars are hazardous enough by their very presence. Don't invite accidents by flouting traffic rules or disregarding basic safe riding practices.

Riding with Children

Before you allow them to ride bikes in the public thoroughfare, have your children practice the same braking, shifting, and riding maneuvers you did. Toward this end, bike rodeos for kids are often sponsored by schools and police groups. They are great practice for young riders. Whenever riding with children, always have them ride ahead of you. You can easily monitor their behavior and shout out corrections.

Riding in traffic requires vigilance. Not only do you need to constantly appraise the road surface for hazards, but you must also be aware of the cars ahead of, beside, and behind you, as well as those crossing, or potentially crossing, your path.

Pedestrians are also a hazard to cyclists. They often underestimate the speed of a bicycle, and will step off the curb directly in front of you. They also are looking for cars, not bikes, so often will not see cyclists. You should assume that any pedestrian standing on the curb will be stepping off the curb in front of you. A bell is a great preventive measure.

Bike lanes are configured in many ways. This bike lane in Minneapolis puts the riders between the curb and parked cars.

Negotiating Intersections

Intersections are very dangerous for cyclists. Motorists are often intent on getting through an intersection before the light changes or ahead of oncoming traffic. Motorists either don't see cyclists or misjudge the speed of cyclists and turn in front of them. A common, and sometimes deadly, accident is the so-called right hook. A cyclist riding on the right side of the road is cut off at an intersection by a motorist turning right. Some towns have painted bike boxes at intersections to limit this occurrence. At these intersections, cars must stop behind the square box and cannot turn right on red. Whether or not this has diminished incidents is not clear. What is clear is that you must be especially tuned in to the vehicles around you when traveling through intersections.

It is important to plan ahead when approaching intersections where you need to turn. There are many scenarios for intersections in downtown zones. The most important concept is that the arc of your turn should take you into your destination lane without crossing traffic lanes. That means that if you are turning left onto a two-way street where you want to end up on the right side of the curb lane, you should line up for your turn in the right portion of the left turn lane. If you are turning left onto a one-way street where you want to end up in the left side of the left lane, you should line up to the left side of the left turn lane. The purpose of this is to not only allow traffic to move past you as you turn, but also to protect you from the rushing left turners who may run you down in their haste.

If you are in a bike lane, obviously you will ride directly up to stop signs and stop lights. If a long line of cars is backed up at a stoplight, you could ride along the curb or shoulder to the front of the line if the road is wide enough and cars can easily pass you without slowing or swerving. But if the road is narrow and all the cars in front of you have already passed you once, it's probably best to stay in line. It never pays to aggravate drivers on narrow roads when they have to pass you multiple times.

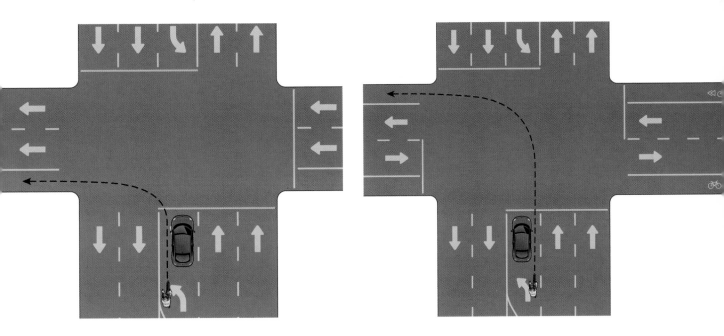

Riding with a Group

Riding with a group is fun. It is also a prime scenario for accidents of the bike-on-bike kind. If you watch professional bike races, you will see that even riders of that level have momentary lapses of attention or judgment that lead to crashes. Unless you are riding on roads that have been closed to car traffic or on extremely wide bike trails, your group should not be riding more than two abreast. When riding in a group, it is very important to be consistent in speed and positioning. Weaving or wobbling while you fiddle with your water bottle could bring you or a companion to the ground when you touch wheels. Signal, by putting your left hand down, slightly out from your body, palm facing backward if you are going to slow down or stop. Let the rider in front of you know if you are close behind by saying, "I'm with you" or "I'm on you." Signal, by pointing, upcoming road hazards or overhang hazards. Keep your fingers on your brakes at all times—because you cannot clearly see the road ahead, you will have less reaction time. But remember, if you suddenly slam on your brakes, you will pile up the riders behind you. Novice riders riding in groups should maintain distances of at least three or four feet from each other, at minimum.

Practice alone to prepare yourself for group rides. Ride in a perfectly straight line at a constant speed while taking drinks of water or shifting gears. Rather than swerving to avoid small obstacles, stand up on the pedals to soften the blow of a small bump or hole.

Riding with a group can be challenging, but it is almost always fun. Practice your riding consistency before going on group rides.

Know Your Physical Limits

Perhaps the most important aspect of safely riding a bike is to have a realistic sense of how skilled or unskilled a cyclist you truly are. Many people overestimate their abilities, only to find themselves in a dangerous situation. The best thing to do is to stop and think and ask questions. Do you really want to ride in midtown Manhattan on your third day of owning a new bike? And remember that a dangerous situation may arise from any variety of sources. The inexperienced rider who shows up without water bottles to a 50 mile club ride on a hot summer day may not realize the risks involved that go beyond automobiles or helmet use. If you are trying something new, ask someone else who has already done it. They can tell you that riding over the steel deck bridge in the rain at rush hour is suicidal. And remember, you can always, always stop and get off the bike. Sometimes walking your bike is the best option.

If you need to actually stop and take a nap the odds are good that you're pushing yourself a little too hard.

This is a major through street, and many cyclists ride on it even though better options are two blocks or fewer away.

This is the street one block to the south of the major through street shown above. Same time of day, yet much better riding conditions.

This bike path on a converted rail bed is located two blocks north of the major through street. It's a virtual bicycle freeway, with almost no interaction with traffic.

Choose a Safe Route

Choosing a wise cycling route is important for your safety and your enjoyment. Many cyclists make the error of cycling on the same route they would choose for driving. If you drive to work on a major through street, you have chosen that route because it is the best route for a car. The best route for a bike may be totally different.

If you have never been a regular cyclist, you may have never thought about getting from point A to point B without using the highway or other major thoroughfares. The fact is, in many areas good or even great options exist for a peaceful cycling route. The easiest option is often to simply move one block off the major route. Some riders will say, "But I have the right to ride on any street I want." Yes, that is true. But why suck car and bus exhaust, deal with lane changers and impatient drivers, and bicycle haters, when you can usually find a less congested route? The added benefit of side streets is also that the condition of the pavement may be superior to the main roads.

Look at a map of the area where you want to ride. See what options are available for your route. Check your city or county website for bike route maps. Many areas have marked off bike lanes on certain streets. The advantages of bike lanes are two-fold. One is that motorists are guided by painted lines which means they are less likely to drift into your lane, and the other is that motorists are accustomed to seeing cyclists on that route and will be more aware of them. If you are lucky, your city or town may have a dedicated bike path or network of bike paths. These paths usually offer a more direct route, and sometimes provide the only way for cyclists and pedestrians to cross highways or rivers.

If you are planning a commuting route, make sure you do a test ride before your first ride to work day. Just because a route looks good on the map doesn't mean it is realistic. Even using the city bike maps and a web feature like Google Maps for bikes doesn't guarantee a good route choice. A nice ride along a parkway may actually include hills or numerous meanders, while a residential street might be a straight flat ride.

If you are riding in suburban or rural areas, the same ideas apply. You may have to go somewhat more out of your way to find quiet byways, but in many areas it is possible. Local bike clubs usually have mapped out local rides or routes. Check out websites for this information by searching "bicycle trails" or "bicycle routes".

Many maps of bicycle routes have been published. Local maps can help you with your commute and day trips, and national maps can help plan vacation routes. Cyclists and cycling organizations also publish books of maps and routes for rides or multi-day tours. Most states have web pages or published material related to bicycling options. Even if you have lived in an area for a long time, you may be surprised at the options available for good cycling.

Some rural highways have nice wide shoulders that are perfect for cycling.

Riding on Sidewalks

Riding on sidewalks is prohibited in most urban areas or business districts, with good reason. No one is going to be satisfied if you are riding on the sidewalk—you can't ride very fast because of the pedestrian hazard, and pedestrians do not want to see a bicycle bearing down on them at speed. Sidewalk riding is best left to children under close adult supervision.

Bridges and Underpasses

Underpasses, overpasses, and bridges are typical pinch points for bicycle routes. Some are traversable only by sidewalk. In these instances, slow down and be prepared to walk your bike. Cyclists do not have the right of way on sidewalks and pedestrians should not be expected to jump aside to let cyclists zoom past. If heavy traffic is an issue, look for other routes. Sometimes lesser-used crossings can be incorporated in a route without making it much longer.

Kids under adult supervision are the only riders who should be cycling on a sidewalk. Limit this usage to residential areas and be on constant lookout for cars backing up in driveways.

This bridge has a bike lane marked next to the right traffic lane. Bridges and underpasses that do not have a bike lane present a challenge to cyclists. The best solution is to dismount and walk your bike across in the pedestrian passageway.

Gallery of Bike Trails and Lanes

Bike lanes come in just about any imaginable shape and location. Even the signage varies tremendously. The most important thing to remember about bike lanes is to use them whenever you can.

• SECURITY

How do you protect your bike investment? Whether you paid $25 or $2500, you want your bike to be there when you leave work or the grocery store. Keeping bikes secure is a primary concern of many cyclists. You also need to consider your personal safety as well.

Bike Locks

Like everything else for cycling, there are multiple choices in the lock department. Balance your local bike theft rate against what you are willing to do and spend to keep your investment safe. Some areas are notorious for bike thievery—around universities for example. If you will be regularly locking your bike in high bike theft areas, you have a number of options in addition to the standard lock.

Remember that anything that is detachable from your bike is likely to be taken. Some people just can't resist removing detachable items, even though they can't use that cycle computer without the hardware. So, begin by taking all those items with you when you leave your bike. If your bike has a quick release seat post, consider replacing the cam lever with a regular bolt. The same is true for quick release hubs. You can purchase skewer locks of all varieties so you don't have to remove your front tire when locking up your bike.

The lock you choose should have the least amount of play or leeway when you have secured your bike to a bike rack. The more leeway there is in the locking mechanism, the more opportunity there is for a thief to pry or cut the lock. The best choice is a U-style lock for securing the frame to a rack, coupled with a cable lock to secure the wheels so you don't have to constantly take the front wheel on and off.

The easiest solution for some of us may be to have more than one bike. A clunker with no quick-release parts is unlikely to be the target for a knowledgeable thief looking for some cash for spendy bike parts. Locking the clunker with a U-style lock usually works. An ugly paint job helps, too.

It probably took this thief one second to pop the quick release and disappear with an almost complete bike.

Many people wonder if it is really necessary to lock the wheels when running into the store for just a minute. The answer is yes.

Bike Lockers

In some bicycle-friendly cities you'll find bike lockers for rent at train or transit stations. Bike lockers are great because no one can see if there is a bike inside or not. Very few thieves are going to work their way through a row of bike lockers in hopes that they find a bike before getting caught. There are way too many easy targets out there.

Some employers allow bicycles to be brought on premises. This is by far the safest option, but probably the least available. The most compact of the folding bikes can easily fit under a desk in a cubicle, completely eliminating worry about bike theft.

Personal Security

Urban life has its down sides, and one is that your personal safety may be threatened by others at times. Just as you are savvy when you drive or walk, be savvy when you bike.

In the nighttime, bike trails can be a hangout for unsavory characters looking to mug an unsuspecting cyclist. The isolation that makes a dedicated bike trail great for a ride also makes it ripe for criminal activity. Fortunately, incidents are fairly rare—but you certainly don't want to be a victim. If you regularly ride a trail, it pays to stay linked in to the local cycling blogs to see if any areas are getting dicey. Choosing to ride streets rather than a trail at night might be a better option. Try to ride with others in small groups. Pepper spray is an effective deterrent if you have it readily available and can dispense it without crashing.

Some cities provide bike lockers for rent near transit stops.

CHAPTER 4

Clothes and Accessories

You don't need any special clothing to ride a bike. But you will find that the more you do ride, the more you may wish you had biking specific gear. Non-cyclists often wonder about the tight black shorts and the bright colored cycling jerseys bicyclists wear. Since these outfits look a bit odd for everyday wear, novice cyclists wonder what the appeal is, but these accessories do serve a purpose.

Accessorizing, whether with clothing or equipment, is a fun and functional way to expand your cycling experience. Some basic accessories are indispensable: these include bottle cages and water bottles. Others, such as handlebar-mounted GPS are fun and appealing and, with little effort, you can probably concoct a scenario where they would be critically useful.

A well-stocked bike shop has a full complement of accessories on hand and ready for purchase.

Performance, exercise, recreation... whatever your cycling objective, choosing appropriate clothing will enhance your experience.

● CLOTHING

Specialized shorts, shirts, tights, and outerwear are available for cycling. These pieces are made of advanced, high-tech fabrics that wick away sweat and repel rain, support muscles and allow for range of movement. And most of them will proudly proclaim your support for a local bike club, brewery, charity ride, or pro team. Plainer clothing is also available.

Bike Shorts

Form-fitting bike shorts provide support to the muscles of the upper leg, and stay in place without bunching or binding during pedaling. Cycling shorts have padding to ease the ride and prevent chafing. Seams are located away from delicate areas, and are flat-stitched to prevent irritation. Black is the most popular color because it doesn't show grease—after re-seating a chain or changing a flat, it is convenient to wipe greasy hands on one's black shorts. These shorts are made of Lycra or some similar material, and the heavier the weight of the fabric, the more compression they apply and the longer they wear.

The stretch fabric allows for full range of movement while on the bike. If you ride a lot, or ride very hard, you will notice that your upper legs swell by the end of your ride. Bike shorts will stretch to accommodate this. The shorts also remain stretchy when wet with sweat, unlike other fabrics that will stick and bind when wet.

Options for gaining the padding advantage without the revealing fit are available. Compression underwear with padding can be worn under any shorts or pants. Two part shorts contain a padded, tight underlayer, and a baggier over layer. Mountain biking shorts are usually two layers, with the outer layer providing abrasion resistance.

If you ride for more than an hour or two at a time, you may benefit from investing in cycling shorts. Also note that cycling shorts are meant to be worn without underwear. Wearing underwear with cycling shorts negates the wicking capabilities of the fabric and the specific non-chafing design of the shorts.

Cycling shorts range in price from $30 to $200. If you don't throw them in the dryer, they can last for years.

Biking shorts are cut to eliminate bunching while in the riding position. MTB shorts have an abrasion resistant outer layer over a padded liner.

Bike Tights

Any sort of athletic tight is nice to wear on a chilly ride. Cycling tights are most often worn over cycling shorts, but you can find tights that have padding and are meant to be worn alone. Tights with wind resistant material on the front are nice.

Leg warmers (not like the ones in Flash Dance!) are also an option. Bike leg warmers cover the leg from the ankles to the bottom of the bike short. They take up less space in your bag if you are traveling light.

Bike Jerseys

Bright colored cycling jerseys are made to fit the cyclist riding in the down position. The sleeves are set slightly forward, and the back of the jersey is cut longer to cover the low back. Jerseys usually have pockets at the lower back, which is very convenient for carrying snacks or a wallet, since bike shorts usually don't have pockets. Jerseys are made of wicking materials and range from $20 to $150. Retro jerseys made of wool are also available. Wool was long the standard for athletic wear because of its wicking properties and because it keeps the wearer warm even when wet. New fabric technology allows for wool to be machine washed, so if you're not a fan of petroleum-derived fibers, wool is an excellent natural option.

A cycling jersey is not an absolute necessity. Many cyclists have ridden thousands of miles without ever donning a jersey. While shorts are crucial to comfort and worth the expense, jerseys are nice to look at and the pockets are convenient, but any shirt made of wicking material is sufficient for most cyclists. Regular cotton T-shirts are okay, but they get heavy and sticky when saturated with sweat. It is also more likely that you will get chilled when wearing cotton.

Riding in a Skirt

Yes, those ladies in the 1800s rode in voluminous skirts. Today's skirts don't have as much yardage, which makes riding easier. Riding in a longer skirt like a dress skirt or peasant skirt requires that your bike have, at minimum, a chain guard. A skirt guard, which is a plastic shield that covers the wheel between the seat stays and chain stays, is also a good idea. Athletic skirts and skorts won't get caught in the chain, but you might find they get caught on the seat.

Cycling jerseys have zippers for ventilation and pockets for wallets, snacks, and maps. Retro wool jerseys are now available in machine washable blends.

Rain and Cold Weather Gear

Biking in the rain or cold weather can be miserable. Wearing the right gear for the conditions makes the experience more tolerable. Finding the right level of waterproofing versus breathability is tricky. Some riders find that sweating from wearing windproof and waterproof raingear is just as drenching as the rain itself. Rain gear often has a variety of ventilation schemes such as pit-zips, zip off sleeves, and double zippers to cope with the issue of overheating.

Because you generate your own wind chill when biking, cold weather riding can be a very chilly activity. Ears, hands, and feet suffer the most, as they are least protected. Earmuffs, balaclavas, neck gaiters, hats, neoprene or windproof gloves and booties are all items available to cyclists.

When choosing cycling outerwear, the more garish the color the better. The neon pinks and yellows are visible at great distance and help set you apart from the background. Reflective piping, tape, or logos are also helpful.

Winter biking is a pursuit that has its own distinct set of requirements, especially when it comes to sportswear. However, interest in cold-weather cycling is making more warm clothing options available for recreational cyclists who simply have little tolerance for cold.

Rain jackets for biking have extra long tails. Many come with zip off sleeves for temperature control.

Gloves

Some cyclists always ride with gloves, and some cyclists never ride with gloves. The main purpose of cycling gloves is to provide padding to the heel of the hand, which is bearing the brunt of the upper body's weight on the handlebars. If you ride an upright bike, this may not be a problem for you. Gloves also protect the palms of your hands if you fall. If you have ever had to pick asphalt bits from the palms of your hands, you know that gloves are a valuable accessory.

Cold- or wet-weather riding requires gloves of some sort. Full-fingered gloves are available with or without insulation. Lobster claw mitts, which group pinkie and ring finger together, and index and middle finger together, allow you to grip brake levers safely, but provide extra warmth by grouping the fingers.

Regular cycling gloves (bottom right) don't have fingertips but they do have padding to protect the palms. Cold weather versions (top right) have palm padding, full fingers and are insulated. Lobster claw mitts (left) make it easy to brake while keeping fingers very toasty.

Bike gloves should provide protection for the heel and palm of your hand without contributing to overheating. Most have no fingertips and are ventilated.

Bicycling shoes are available in walkable styles (left) for multi-purpose use, or in racing styles (right) suitable only for on-bike use.

Bike Shoes

You can cycle in just about any type of shoe, but some are definitely better than others for the job. Ideally, your biking shoes should be secured to your feet—clogs and flip-flops are poor cycling choices. The laces should be as short as possible. Shoes that are specially made for cycling are very rigid. In fact, racing shoes have no flexibility at all. If you have ridden a long way in running shoes with rattrap pedals, you may appreciate how a rigid shoe might be helpful. It is inefficient to use leg power to push down on a squishy shoe over and over, plus squishy shoes lead to sore feet. A rigid shoe transfers more power to the pedal, while distributing the pedal pressure over more of your foot.

Bike shoes for use with toe clips and straps are difficult to find, as fewer people still use the toe clip option. Shoes for clipless pedals come in a variety of options ranging from racing shoes at hundreds of dollars a pair, to sport shoes for under fifty dollars. Dedicated racing shoes are not suitable for walking. You may have seen bikers wearing these shoes awkwardly walking around the coffee shop before or after their team ride. A better option for most of us is shoes that can be used on and off the bike. These shoes are rigid and have the same clipless cleat systems, but have tread and heels so you can walk normally. You can even get sandals with clipless cleats. You can use clipless shoes without the cleats. Just be careful if you are using toe clips. Make sure your shoes can easily slide out off the pedal and out of the straps. If you want to fully use the clipless cleat system, you need to purchase the pedals, shoes, and shoe cleats. The pedals can be found for as low as $40 or $50 from online vendors. The shoe cleats cost around $20 and the shoes range from $50 to $300.

If you are in the market for some dedicated bike shoes, there are a number of brands of clipless systems from which you can choose. Five major systems are SPD (Shimano Pedaling Dynamics), LOOK, Time, Crankbrothers, and Speedplay. Shoes, pedals, and cleats are not interchangeable between these systems, and sometimes are not even interchangeable within the proprietary systems. Always double-check shoes and pedals for compatibility before purchasing. Note that you can only use these pedals if you have the shoes and cleats to fit them. Street shoes will not work with these pedals. For casual riders the SPD system offers the most options. The SPD system also has a double-sided pedal that can be used with cleats or with street shoes.

If you decide to ride with either toe clips or a clipless cleat system, make sure you practice, practice, practice. To remove your foot from standard toe clips, simply pull your foot straight back. To unclip from clipless pedals, turn your heel sharply to the outside. Clipping in usually involves sliding the toe of the cleat in first, then pushing down on the heel. All systems are slightly different, however, so read the directions carefully. Always begin with the resistance set on the easiest release setting. The inability to unclip quickly and automatically has caused even experienced cyclists to tumble over. It is embarrassing and painful.

If you replace the pedals on your bike, note that the pedal marked L is for the left side of the bike, and the pedal marked R is for the right side. The left pedal is left hand threaded, meaning it tightens to the left, or counterclockwise. The right pedal tightens to the right, as usual.

Clipless pedals come in a variety of configurations. Cleats designed to match the clip hardware are screwed onto the shoes to complete the system. Types shown above include (left): Crankbrothers, (middle): LOOK, (right): Shimano.

Some accessories, such as a water bottle with a mounting cage on the bike frame, are virtually mandatory if you'll be going on trips in excess of 20 minutes long.

● ACCESSORIES

Loads of accessories are available for bicycles. You can trick out your adult bike with all kinds of racks, bags, baskets, computers, and mirrors. The effect may not be as memorable as a playing card clothespinned to a spoke, or as dazzling as handlebar streamers, but accessorizing your bike (and yourself) is a pursuit most cyclists enjoy.

Bottle Cages and Bottles

Water bottles are a necessity if you will be riding for more than twenty minutes at a time. Most bikes come with the attachment points (braze-ons) for one or two bottle cages, though some comfort bikes have none. Cages are made of aluminum or plastic, and are fairly inexpensive. Buy as many cages as your bike has attachment points. They are the least expensive accessory, but definitely highest in value.

Water bottles are designed to fit in the bottle cages. They have a spout so you can squeeze water into your mouth without having to remove a cap. Look for bottles that have soft rubber spouts (they are easier to pull open with your teeth) and large screw off caps for easier cleaning and to allow for adding ice cubes. Insulated bottles are also available.

Backpack based hydration systems are widely available, and very popular. These packs hold anywhere from 40 to 100 ounces of water. A tube with a bite valve clips to the front of your shirt so you can get a hands-free drink anytime. The packs also have pockets for carrying keys, phones, and treats. Their only drawbacks are that they can make you hotter while you are riding, and keeping the pouches clean requires meticulous attention due to their propensity to mildew.

Bottle cages and bicycling water bottles make it easier to keep hydrated. A backpack hydration system can carry large amounts of water and the drinking tube allows hands-free drinking.

Bike Pumps

A portable bike pump is a good idea if you are riding longer distances or in more remote areas. Most pumps have a method for attaching to the bike frame, though some are compact enough to easily fit in a handlebar bag. Don't forget you'll also need a spare tube or a patch kit! Virtually all pumps now have adaptors to fit either Presta or Schrader valves. Make sure you have set the pump up to fit your bike tires before you go on the road.

Bicycle Computers

Cycling computers use sensors to report how fast the bike is going, how fast you are pedaling, and, with additional sensors, your heart rate. Other features include timers, altimeters, cumulative miles, and trip times. Of course, now brackets are available to attach smartphones or GPS systems to handlebars.

A tire pump of some sort is a necessity. Most cyclists have a floor pump for home use and a frame or bag pump to carry on the bike.

The Presta valve has become very popular for bicycle inner tube valves. A pump that's configured for the old style valves (called Schrader valves) will not fit onto a Presta. Make sure your tire pump has a Presta adapter, as your next replacement inner tube will likely have this type of fitting.

Handlebar Bags

A handlebar bag is an excellent first choice in bike bags. A handlebar bag can hold your route maps (some have clear map pouches), your phone, some snacks, and your tire patch kit. It's all easily accessible right at your fingertips. They come in sizes small to large, so it's easy to get the size and features you need. Bags come with a variety of attachment systems geared toward different bar styles, so it's good to take your bike with you when shopping for handlebar bags.

Seat Bags

Seat bags are small bags that strap to the seat rails and seat post. They are the perfect size for a spare tire, tire levers, patch kit, and folding combo tool. They are inexpensive and easy to detach, so they work well as a basic first bag. Racers like these bags because they don't add to the aerodynamic drag.

Bike Racks

A rear rack is very useful if you use your bike for commuting or shopping. Choices include a seat-post-mounted rack or a rack that bolts to the chain stays and seat stays. Some racks come with a spring-loaded clip for securing items. Some racks are designed to work together with certain bags or rack trunks. Racks are not typically designed to carry passengers or to have a child seat mounted to them, and they have a recommended maximum weight restriction. The seat-post-mounted racks have the lowest weight limits. These racks are great for a small rack trunk on a mountain bike, especially one with rear suspension, but using panniers with this type of rack creates the possibility of spoke entanglement when panniers move around due to rough roads. This is not a good situation.

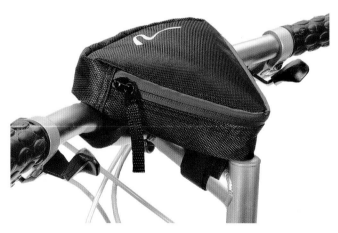

A handlebar bag is a useful first bag. Everything is within reach, and many have a clear map case to keep your route handy.

Seat bags provide quick, accessible storage and are also inexpensive.

Rear racks with weight ratings of 40 to 50 pounds are available to fit most bikes. It is helpful to bring your bike along when you shop for a rack, as some bikes are not as easy to fit as others. Rack styles are changing rapidly as manufacturers have introduced new models for cruiser style bikes and other hard-to-fit frames.

Front racks are also available. Low riding front racks actually provide for the best load balance, but it is rare that you will see anyone riding with these racks unless they are a cycle tourist.

Baskets

As with racks, you'll find that the basket choices are increasing all the time. How about a nice wicker basket for your handlebars? Or a basket with an insulated liner to keep your ice cream chilly on the ride home? Or grocery-bag-sized baskets for a rear rack that fold up when not in use. These baskets and more are available from many sources. Baskets are very convenient for short-trip transporting because you don't have to secure your items to a rack: you simply toss them in. Another plus is that baskets are either bolted on so you don't have to worry about them being stolen, or they are attached with quick release features so you can pop them off and take them with you.

If possible, bring your bike with you to the bike shop when you look for a basket. Some baskets may fit great on one bike but very awkwardly on another. If you buy online, take the time to read some reviews to see if others have encountered fit problems.

If you ride regularly and have bolt-on baskets, check the bolt tightness periodically. Most bolts come with a little thread tightener applied, or with locking nuts, but it pays to keep an eye on these connections.

It is a good idea to secure items in a basket with an elasticized cargo net. Hitting a big bump can send everything flying out of a basket.

Fenders

Why don't bikes come with fenders? That's a good question and often asked by cyclists over age 45 who remember all their childhood bikes having had fenders. The ten-speed revolution of the 1970s killed the fender in the U.S. Since we are not a nation of bicycle commuters, a la the Netherlands, our bikes get used for outings on nice weekends, not daily rides to work through every kind of weather. Manufacturers can save that little bit by not installing fenders, and after-market manufacturers can make a little bit by selling us some fenders.

If you commute regularly, and don't live in the desert, get a set of fenders. Even if you don't regularly leave the house to ride to work on rainy days, you will get caught in the rain eventually, and wet pavement and puddles will be around for a while after it rains. Fenders also cut down on the amount of sand and dirt that are thrown up onto your legs and chain.

If you don't want bolt-on fenders, quick release versions that attach to the seat post or snap on to the down tube are available. They stop some of the grit and spray from hitting you.

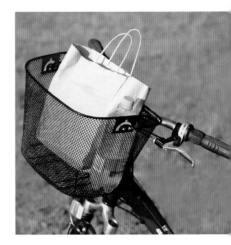

Handle-mounted baskets are handy because they allow easy access during short trips. To keep items from flying out during longer trips, secure them with a cargo net.

Fenders are popular aftermarket bike accessories. They come in a variety of styles, materials, and attachment methods. Some are intended to be installed permanently, others, like the one above, can be snapped on easily if the weather is threatening.

Panniers

Panniers are bicycle bags that mount onto a rear or front rack. Panniers range in size from small to huge and most are designed for bicycle touring. Most panniers have a hook that attaches to the bottom of the rack, and two hooks that clip onto the top of the rack. Panniers are difficult for everyday use because they are not grocery bag size, so you have to repack your items, and they are usually somewhat oddly shaped. The larger, more squared panniers are good for carrying a change of clothes and lunch if you are a commuter.

Some panniers are created especially for commuters. They look a little like a garment bag, and fold over the top of the rear rack like a saddlebag. The advantage is that suits and dresses do not get as wrinkled when they are carefully packed into this style of pannier.

Panniers designed for grocery shopping are sized to hold a grocery bag or are designed with handles and a quick release system so you can pop them off, shop, load the panniers, and pop them back on.

Panniers, at least as they are known in the U.S., are essentially saddle bags that straddle your rear tire.

Rack Trunks

Rack trunks are storage bags that mount on the rear rack. Some are insulated, which makes them perfect for carrying picnic supplies. Larger rack trunks are suitable for carrying work clothes, if you don't mind folded clothes, but taking the trunk on and off can be a bit of a hassle unless you get the integrated rack-trunk quick release systems.

Panniers attach to the front or rear racks and are available in a wide range of sizes.

Backpacks and Bags

Riding with backpacks is very common. Since most of us already have an old frameless backpack lying around somewhere, it doesn't require any investment. Backpacks have two main drawbacks for cyclists. One is that they increase your heat factor. The other is that they increase the amount of weight above the bike's center of gravity. For inexperienced riders this can increase wobbliness. However, backpacks are safer for riding than messenger bags.

Messenger bags are cool, but perhaps not the most practical. If you ride with one, use the auxiliary strap around your waist. Otherwise the bag can move a bit too freely and cause a distraction. Unless you have a very large bag, they don't hold much. Be careful with messenger bags. Make sure the strap is short enough that the bag rides well above your waist. If the bag rides below your waist it can get caught under the seat as you mount. The sudden jerky stop as the bag catches under the seat as you are attempting to move forward is very entertaining to the people sitting outside the coffee shop, but not very pleasant for the cyclist.

Mirrors

Some cyclists swear by mirrors, some say they are terribly distracting. Whatever style mirror you use, there will be a learning curve involved—it isn't as straight forward as car mirrors for some reason. Mirror options include small, dental sized mirrors that attach to eyeglasses or helmets, and larger mirrors that attach to handlebars. Handlebar attachments might be bolt-on or end-of-tube style.

Mirrors are not a substitute for a good look over the shoulder, but they do allow you to be more aware of your surroundings. Mirrors are especially helpful for rural road or bike path riding. On rural roads, mirrors allow you to see large vehicles approaching long before you hear them. On bike paths, mirrors allow you to see the silent cyclist who is approaching from behind at double your speed.

TIP

Bells

Bells are good alert devices to let pedestrians or slower bikes know you're passing. Telling a pedestrian that you're "On Your Left" sometimes results in them jumping to the left, directly into your path. A bell usually results in a less violent response.

Rear-view mirrors can be mounted to your handlebars or to your helmet.

A standard-issue, frameless backpack has more capacity and is safer for beginning riders to use than fancier bike packs, such as messenger packs.

A trunk style rack often works on a van.

If you are interested in mountain biking, a bike rack and a utility vehicle are your ticket to the most remote trails.

Roof racks may have struts to hold the bike on with both wheels in place, or quick release levers to hold the fork in place with the front wheel removed.

CAR RACKS

If you want to do some cycling away from home, and you don't have a large vehicle, a car rack is a must. Fortunately they come in a range of styles, some of which are fairly inexpensive. Options for rack mounting points include trunk, hitch, spare tire, truck bed, and roof.

The trunk-mounted racks are typically the least expensive and are good for trips long or short. Most trunk racks easily hold two bikes (they may say that they hold three, but this can be tricky to accomplish). If you have a bike with a step-through frame, you need to buy an adapter that clamps to the handlebars and seat post that makes the bike suitable for fitting the rack. Bikes mounted on a trunk rack can obscure taillights or license plates. It can be disconcerting to watch your bike bounce around on these types of racks, but if you regularly check for strap tightness (especially after rain) they are absolutely secure. A major disadvantage of the trunk rack is that you do not have access to the trunk contents while the rack is on the car. This is highly irritating if you have a flat tire or a coffee spill and need a fresh change of clothes.

Many cyclists prefer roof racks because the bike is very securely attached with mechanical locking fasteners and not fabric straps. Roof racks don't interfere with trunk access, and many of them have lockable car top carrier pods available to increase storage space. If you participate in other outdoor sports like kayaking, canoeing, or skiing, roof racks are a great option. Roof racks tend to be more expensive. Two major disadvantages of roof racks are that you have to be able to lift your bike on and off the roof, and you need to remember that your bike is mounted on your roof before you drive into your garage or a parking garage. Wind noise and increased aerodynamic drag are other drawbacks of the roof racks.

If you have an SUV, the spare tire mount is nice because you can often open the back without removing the rack. These racks are very securely mounted to the spare tire mounts (with the tire on).

Hitch racks can accommodate up to five bikes. They are a good option if you already have a vehicle with a trailer hitch. They work best on vehicles with more ground clearance, as they project behind the vehicle somewhat and can scrape on driveways and speed bumps.

Truck bed mounts can either be bars that mount across the side panels, or bolt into the truck bed.

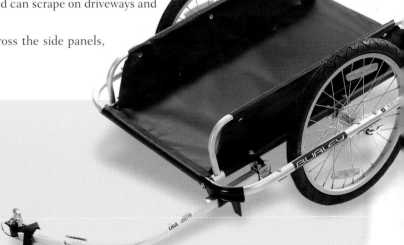

Bike Trailers

Bike trailers are not trailers for hauling bikes, but trailers to pull with a bike. Bike trailers are great for hauling kids and lots of stuff. There are two major varieties—one with seats for kids (or pets), or one for things.

CHAPTER 5

The Bicycle: An Overview

Everyone knows what a bike looks like, right? Two wheels, pedals, chain, handlebars, and a seat, plus a frame to hold it all together. It's true. Bicycles are really rather simple. For the most part, the casual rider doesn't need to know too much about how a bicycle has been designed and manufactured or how all the pieces work together.

On the other hand, bicycles are simple enough that most of us benefit from a bit of technical information. You can use the information in this section to familiarize yourself with the terms you will hear while shopping for a bike. Or you can simply use it as a reference section for when you might have questions in the future.

An interesting note about bicycles is that most bicycle manufacturers only really design and make the frame. The components—brakes, derailleurs, pedals, chains, sprockets, wheels—are manufactured by a small number of component makers. Regardless of the brand on the bike frame, almost every bike you look at will have components made by Shimano or SRAM or one or two other companies. Bicycle manufacturers decide which level of component to match with each frame design to create a bike targeted at a certain user and price point. Within the same price range, you will find most bicycles will have the same component group.

The components are also very similar, even if manufactured by different companies. A front derailleur looks like a front derailleur looks like a front derailleur. This is a plus because you have fewer decisions to make, and if you choose to do maintenance work there is little variation from bike to bike.

• PARTS OF A BIKE

The following information about the broad subject of bicycle parts covers both the general and the more specific. When you shop for a bike, you may encounter a salesperson who likes to toss off technical bike terms. It is nice to have a basic understanding of the terms; however, if you are a casual rider you honestly don't need to know what any of the terms mean.

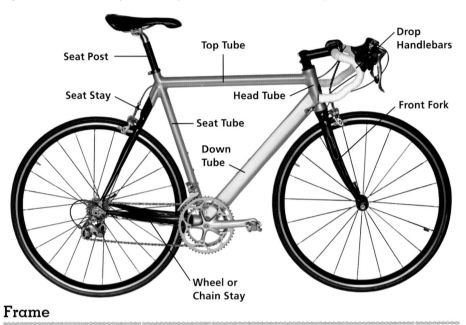

Frame

The frame is the metal structure that all the other parts are attached to. Frames are typically steel or aluminum, though they may also be made of titanium or carbon fiber. Each material has advantages and disadvantages. Aluminum is very lightweight and rigid, but that creates a somewhat harsh ride. Steel and carbon frames have a balance of rigidity and flex, so the ride is not so jolting. Carbon and titanium are very lightweight, but also very expensive.

The mixte frame is stronger than the standard step-through frame.

On an upright style bicycle, either mountain bike or road bike, the frame has roughly a diamond shape. Recumbent bike frames are often a single bar. Some frames may have a straight top tube (the old boys' bike) or a step through frame (the old girls' bike). Some bikes have a mixte frame, which looks like half way between the straight and step through frames. Many frames today are based on a mountain bike style where the top tube slopes downward toward the seat tube.

Back in the Old Days, when all bikes had the same frame geometry (the diamond), it was easy to compare sizes because a 20" frame on one bike was virtually the same size as a 20" frame on another bike. The measurement refers to the length of the seat tube. With the many different frame configurations today, the seat tube measurement is less relevant. A road bike with a 20" frame may fit you, but a mountain bike that is the correct size for you may only have a 15" frame.

Metal frames are made from metal tubing that has been cut and welded together. A lugged frame means that special brackets have been made to fit around the tube junctions. This makes for a very strong joint. Butted tubing is tubing that is thicker at the ends and thinner in the middle. This makes it stronger with less weight. Braze-ons are threaded nubs that have been brazed (a type of soldering) onto the frame to serve as attachment points for brakes, derailleurs, cables, racks, fenders, pumps, and bottle cages.

The frame parts are the seat tube, which the seat post slides into, the head tube, which the front fork slides into, and the top tube which connects these two. The tube between the head tube and the base of the seat tube is the down tube. Where the seat tube and the down tube meet is the bottom bracket which holds the spindle and bearings for the crank set. Holding the rear wheel are the wheel stays and seat stays.

The standard frame is an immobile structure (although some frames have suspension elements, which allow the rear wheel to move up and down). Each frame is intended to work with a specific wheel size and width. You have some leeway in terms of wheel width, but the frame will only fit one wheel diameter.

Flat Handlebars

Top Tube

Suspension Fork

Rear Suspension

Down Tube

Front Fork

The front fork is not technically considered part of the frame, because it is not permanently attached. The fork slides into the head tube and is attached with a locking mechanism. Two sets of ball bearings allow the fork to move freely in the tube, while being able to support a great deal of weight. This pair of bearings is called the headset. Some forks are straight and some are curved (raked). The rake of the front fork is important to handling and comfort.

Forks may be made of different materials than the frame. An aluminum bike may have a steel fork to somewhat soften the ride.

Suspension forks are increasingly common, even on non-mountain bikes. The suspension provides two benefits. One is that your hands don't take such a beating if you are bouncing over rocks and tree roots on a trail, or potholes on a rough road. The other is that the shock absorption keeps the front tire in contact with the ground, which increases handling.

A suspension fork on a mountain bike absorbs much of the shock so it doesn't transmit to the rider's hands. Suspension forks also can be installed on hybrid bikes to make rough commutes more comfortable.

A typical front wheel has spokes laced together and anchored in the hub and the rim.

Wheel

At the center of each wheel is an axle within a hub. Two sets of ball bearings allow the wheel to turn smoothly and two sets of locking bolts hold the axle and bearing assemblies within the hub. Quick release wheels have a hollow axle through which a long pin and cam mechanism are threaded. The quick release allows you to remove the wheel without any tools. A standard axle is threaded and is attached to the frame or fork with nuts.

The spokes are threaded through holes in the hub and are held in place by a flattened end. The spokes are threaded at the rim end and are held in place with special nuts called spoke nipples. Spokes come in different thicknesses (called gauge), and wheels have different numbers of spokes. How the spokes are arranged is called the lacing pattern. The spokes are arranged, or laced, in specific patterns from the hub to the rim. You will see that some wheels have very few spokes that do not cross each other while other wheels have many spokes that cross two or even three times. Lacing patterns, spoke materials, and spoke gauge affect the weight and strength of a wheel. All the spokes on a wheel are tensioned precisely to hold the rim in perfect alignment. This is called true. A wobbly wheel is out of true, and can be trued by a process of loosening and tightening the spoke nipples.

Rims are typically made of aluminum, though older or less expensive bikes may have steel rims. Rims come in many widths. A mountain bike rim or cruiser bike rim may be an inch or more wide. A rim for a road-racing bike may be a scant ¾ inch.

Around the rims on the inside is a piece of plastic or rubber called rim tape. This prevents the spoke nipples from puncturing the inner tube.

Wheel Size

Wheels come in many sizes. The diameter of the rim is one dimension, and the width of the rim is the other. One rim width can usually accommodate a range of tire widths. For example, a one-inch rim can accommodate tires from 1 to 1½" wide. The tire diameter, however, must match the rim diameter exactly.

A quick-release lever lets you remove a front or rear wheel without using any tools. The intent is to allow you to quickly pop the wheel off to change a tire.

Tires

Tires are sized to fit rim diameter as well as width. Dimensions are given as diameter × width. So a 27 × 1¼ inch tire fits a 27-inch wheel and it is 1¼ inch wide. A 700 × 23 tire fits a 700c wheel and has a width of 23 mm. Tires can have a smooth tread (slick) or very pronounced tread (knobby) and everything in between. Slick tires are good for riding on paved surfaces. Knobby tires are good for riding on loose dirt and gravel, where their additional texture grabs well. Riding on pavement with knobby tires is loud and takes much more energy than cruising along pavement on your slicks.

Tires must be used with inner tubes, which are sized to fit specific tire diameters and a range of widths.

The majority of bike tires are called clinchers. They have wire or Kevlar beads, which hold them in place, or clinch them, onto the rims. The advantage of Kevlar over wire beads is that these tires weigh a little bit less, but also they can be folded flat, which is an advantage for carrying a spare tire while touring. Bicycle racers ride on tires called sew-ups or tubular tires. These tires are glued to the rims, so they have no bead.

Inner Tubes

Inner tubes are typically made of rubber, though some puncture-proof varieties are available that incorporate other compounds. Inner tubes come in sizes matched to the diameter of the wheel and the width of the tire. Inner tubes also come matched to the

Bicycle tires are available from fantastically gnarly knobbies to super skinny slicks.

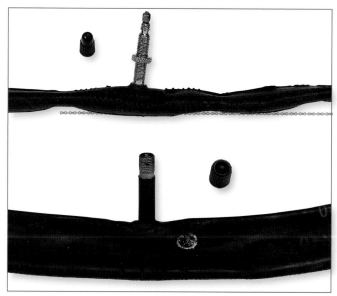

Two styles of valves are found on bicycle inner tubes. The Schrader valve (bottom) is rubber covered and is the same as a car tire valve. The Presta valve (top) is threaded metal and has a locking stem. If you've never used a Presta valve, ask for a demo at your bike shop. They require some explanation.

valve hole that is drilled in the rim. Valves are either Presta or Schrader. Presta valves are thin metal threaded valves with a threaded valve stem. The valve head is unscrewed to open the valve for filling, and screwed down to lock. The Schrader valve looks just like the valve on a car tire—a rubber coated stem with threads for a cap and a valve lock that is activated by a pointed mechanism within the pump head. As you may have guessed, these parts are not interchangeable, and you must use a Presta head pump with a Presta valve and a Schrader head pump with a Schrader valve. Some pumps come with parts that can be flipped to allow use with both valves.

The Seat

Seats, frequently called saddles, come in many shapes and sizes. Seats are leather or vinyl stretched over padding on top of a hard plastic base. You can get seats or seat covers with gel inserts to pad your ride.

Some seats have a cut-out section in the middle, or a groove down the middle. This is to ease pressure on the tailbone and on nerves in the crotch area. Seats are available in men's and women's models. This is because men's and women's sit bones are spaced differently.

The old-fashioned leather saddle is still available, and some riders swear that this is the only saddle to have. These saddles are very thick leather riveted to a metal suspension. This type of saddle needs to be broken in through an intensive process of oiling and riding, and, some say, hammering with a ball-peen hammer. Over years of riding, this saddle will form to your sit bones and truly become a custom seat.

The seat is mounted on the seat post. Seat posts come in a variety of lengths, and slide into the seat tube. Moving the seat post up or down in the seat tube is how you change the height of your riding position. Seat posts are secured with bolts or quick release levers.

Given the wide assortment of saddles available, everyone should find what he or she needs, from retro to racing to leisurely cruising.

Handlebars

Handlebars come in three common configurations, although there are almost unlimited variations to be found. Mountain bike handlebars are usually a flat, straight bar. Bar ends are often installed on these flat handlebars to create more hand positions or allow for more upright riding. Cruisers usually have curved bars with a bit of a rise to them with a single grip area. For a real up high grip, it is still possible to get the old style Sting Ray style handlebars, though they usually don't come as original equipment.

Road bikes have drop bars which curl down and provide numerous hand positions. You may see people zipping by with aero bars. These clamp-on bars jut out from the front of the handle bars and have elbow pads. Using these bars creates a very down, very aerodynamic riding position. Cow horn or mustache bars look like cruiser handlebars that have been turned upside down and pointed forward instead of back. Like drop bars, these bars provide numerous potential hand positions.

Stem

The stem connects the handlebars to the front fork. Stems come in different sizes and configurations. The reach and angle measures how far forward and upward the arm of the stem protrudes. Stems used to be made at sharp or right angles and in one piece. They were clamped inside the fork tube so it could be raised or lowered by loosening the clamp bolt. Now, stems come in many configurations and the stem clamps onto the outside of the fork tube. Spacers on the fork tube adjust the stem height, and typically the fork tube is cut to fit. Some bikes come with adjustable stems to allow for quick adjustment with a hex wrench. Replacing a stem with a shorter or longer reach or angle stem is one way to customize the fit of a bike.

Headset

The headset is the bearing mechanism that attaches the fork to the bike frame and allows the fork to move. Two sets of bearings, one at the top and one at the bottom of the head tube, bear the weight of the cyclist while allowing for steering. Older and less expensive bicycles have threaded headsets. That means the fork has a threaded top that the headset screws on to. Most bicycles now come with threadless headsets. The fork is not threaded, and the headset is held together by a clamping mechanism rather than a threaded nut.

A threaded headset is held in place with a nut, and the stem is called a quill stem and is held in place with an interior clamp.

Most new bikes have a threadless headset. The stem clamps onto the outside of the steerer tube.

Shifters

Shifters are adjusted to change the bike gear. Twist shifts are mounted around the handlebars, and are used by gripping and twisting. Thumb shifters are small levers to be operated by the thumb, or thumb and forefinger. Bar end shifters are small shift levers mounted in the bar ends of drop style handlebars. These are often the choice for tourists, since they are often riding in the down position to decrease wind resistance. Brake shifters are integrated into the brake levers on drop handlebars. The shifters are activated by pushing side to side, or pushing to one side and using a thumb trigger for the other direction.

Shift levers are found on older bikes that used friction shifting. These may be located at the top of the head tube or mounted on the down tube. The levers moved in a continuous smooth motion, and the rider shifted by feel and practice into the desired gear. All new bikes have indexed shifting. The shifter clicks into a series of positions that correlate with a certain gear. Some derailleur systems still use friction shifting for the front derailleur. This is beneficial when using a triple crankset with a 9 or 10 sprocket cassette. Because of the wide gearing range, friction shifting allows for precise adjustment to the front derailleur to prevent the chain from rubbing.

Thumb shifters usually have two levers, one operated by the thumb and one by the forefinger.

Twist shifters are easy to use and are always in hand, which is very safe.

Bar end shifters are popular with those who enjoy touring. The shift levers are conveniently close so that minimal effort is needed for shifting.

Brakes

The most common brakes are called rim brakes and have levers installed on the handlebars. The levers are connected to the brake mechanism with brake cables. Squeezing the levers shortens the cable, which then squeezes rubber brake pads against the wheel rims.

Rim brakes all use a caliper mechanism. The three styles are referred to as caliper, cantilever, or linear pull. Caliper brakes are currently used on road bikes and can be found on most older bikes. This brake looks like a C centered over the tire and rim. The brake attaches to the frame at a single point. Most modern versions are sidepull, dual pivot, but on older ten-speeds sidepull single pivot and centerpull versions were often used. The disadvantage of the caliper brake is that they have little clearance for larger tires or dirt and mud.

Cantilever and linear pull brakes are standard on almost all hybrid and mountain bikes, and some comfort bikes. The cantilever brake has two arms that angle outwards, and the arms are mounted onto posts on the fork or the seat stays. When activated, the center pull cable pulls up the arms which pushes the pads against the rims. These brakes were used on earlier versions of the mountain bike. Linear pull brakes are almost always referred to as V-Brakes, which is the Shimano trademark. Linear pull brakes also have two arms that attach to the forks and seat stays. The brake arms are straighter, and the cable runs through a metal sleeve (noodle) and pulls from the side. The advantage of the cantilever and linear pull brakes is that they allow for wider tires and can apply more braking force.

Also available are disc brakes. Instead of grippers squeezing the tire sidewall, the disc brake operates exactly like a car disc brake. A gripping mechanism with pads squeezes a disc that is mounted around the hub. The advantage of the disc brake is an exponential increase in stopping power, and a system that is not affected by water or mud. Disc brakes may be either hydraulic or cable activated.

A single speed cruiser often has a coaster brake. A coaster brake allows the rider to coast, with the pedals not rotating, or brake by pushing backward on the pedals. Coaster brakes fall into the category of drum brakes, because the brake is contained within the hub. Other drum brakes are activated with a hand lever. The advantage of the drum brake is that it is protected from the elements, so not affected by water. However, drum brakes are very heavy, so are mostly used for casual or cargo bikes.

Road bikes usually have dual-pivot caliper brakes. The brakes have low clearance, so they aren't suitable for fat tires or muddy conditions.

The cantilever brake has clearance for large tires and mud.

Linear pull brakes have good clearance and excellent stopping power.

Disc brakes are very powerful, are not as affected by moisture as rim brakes, and do not require sturdy wheel rims to operate.

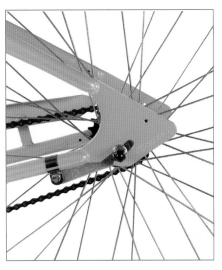

Coaster brakes are not affected by weather because they operate internally.

Most road bikes now have shift levers integrated with brake levers.

Crankset

The crankset is made up of the chainrings, crank arms, and pedals. The crankset mounts onto the spindle arms which project from the bottom bracket. The crankset is the mechanism that converts your muscle power into drive power for your bike.

Chainrings

The chainring or rings are the front sprockets that hold the chain. A bike may have one, two, or three chainrings. Chainrings are sized by number of teeth—53 teeth is very large and 22 teeth is very small. The very small chainrings are referred to as granny gears, either because they have few teeth or because only granny needs to have a chainring this small. Road bikes usually have two chainrings. Mountain bikes, hybrids, and touring bikes are equipped with three chainrings. More chainrings means more gearing options, and for off-road riding, comfort, and long-distance touring, the more options, the better.

The difference between the number of teeth on the two or three chainrings is limited to the ability of the front derailleur to lift the chain up to the next ring. This is the maximum capacity of the derailleur. For older bikes this number was 10, but new derailleurs can handle larger ranges like 16. Older road bikes often came with 52/42t front chainrings. Current road bikes commonly have a 52/39t or a 50/34t set. A mountain bike with a triple chainring might be 44/32/22t.

It is possible to change out chainring sizes, or even to replace a double crankset for a triple crankset. Changing ring sizes is not terribly difficult, but moving from two to three chainrings requires replacing the entire crankset and the front derailleur.

A crank set consists of two crank arms and two or three chainrings. Mountain bike or hybrid cranksets usually have three chainrings, and road bike sets have two.

The classic bicycle
pedal has grippy edges
and rotates on its own axle
after it is screwed to the crank arm.

Toe clips keep the foot
from slipping off the pedal. A
cage only (left) allows for quick exits. A
cage with strap securely attaches the foot to the pedal.

Pedals

The pedals are platforms that spin freely on axles that are threaded into the crank arms. The left pedal has a left hand thread, meaning it tightens to the left, or counterclockwise. Pedals are stamped with an L or R by the threads.

Pedals come in a huge variety of shapes, sizes, and styles. Pedals for casual riding may be wide platforms made of metal or plastic, with some amount of grippy surface to prevent feet from slipping off. Either side of the pedal can be used for riding. Rattrap pedals are metal with points to provide more grip.

A problem with pedals is that the harder or faster you pedal, the more likely it is that your feet will slip off the pedals. A number of options are available to prevent slipping and to maximize the transfer of cranking power. Toe clips and straps create a cage around the foot to prevent forward or side-to-side slipping. Toe clips and straps can be used with any kind of footwear, but they only attach to pedals that have strap slots and bolt holes for clips.

Clipless pedals have an attachment mechanism which interfaces with a cleat attached to biking shoes. There are many manufacturers producing a range of these pedals, cleats, and shoes. Some systems are meant for racing, with shoes that are completely rigid and only suitable for pedaling. Other systems are meant for general riding and have shoes with recessed cleats so you can walk in the shoes. Most clipless pedals are useable only with the cleated shoes, though a few are double sided which allows for any shoe to be used. (See page 73 for photo of clipless pedals and cleats.)

Derailleurs

Derailleurs are the mechanical arms that lift and push the chain between chainrings on the front and sprockets on the cassette in the back. Derailleurs are connected to the shifters with wire cables. Derailleurs work specifically with certain size ranges of chainrings or cassettes.

Front derailleurs all look fairly similar, a simple lever arm with sides that guide the chain side to side and a roller bar to lift the chain up. Rear derailleurs cages may be short or long. The cage is the part of the rear derailleur that contains the two pulleys that the chain runs over. Rear derailleurs move the chain back and forth between sprockets, but also take up the slack chain when using smaller rings, so the rear derailleur is responsible for maintaining chain tension in addition to shifting.

The front derailleur pushes and lifts or drops the chain between chainrings.

Most road bikes have a short cage derailleur because the difference between the highest and lowest gears is small so there is not as much chain slack.

Mountain bikes and many hybrid and comfort bikes have a very wide range of gears. The cage on the derailleur is longer to take up the extra chain length.

Cassette

The cassette is the set of toothed sprockets (also called cogs or gears) attached to the rear wheel. Cassettes are made up of groups of eight to eleven sprockets. Older bikes had five, six, or seven. The cassettes are labeled by the number of teeth on the smallest and largest sprockets. A typical road bike cassette has ten or eleven sprockets ranging from 11 to 23 or 12 to 25. Mountain bikes usually have a larger range, like 11 to 34.

For most cyclists, cassettes are not customizable. Which is fine; cassettes are available in a wide range of combinations set up for road riding or mountain biking. The road cassettes have only a one tooth difference between each sprocket, while the mountain bike, or MTB cassettes may have a larger range in total, or one very large sprocket.

Cassette Freehub or Freewheel

The cassette is attached to the cassette freehub. The freehub is the mechanism that allows you to coast without pedaling, then engage when you pedal forward. Bicycles used to have a mechanism called a freewheel, which was a separate part that threaded onto the hub, but now almost all bicycles come with the integrated freehub.

Internal Gear Hub

An internal gear hub has all the gearing hidden within the hub. Internal gear hubs are available with three to fourteen gears. The advantage of the internal gear hub is that it needs little or no maintenance because the hub is sealed from moisture and dirt. The disadvantage is the high initial price. The nine-speed hub is now used on a number of commuter style bicycles.

Cassettes are the sets of sprockets mounted on the hub of the rear wheel. They are available in sizes and intervals suitable for road racing or mountain climbing.

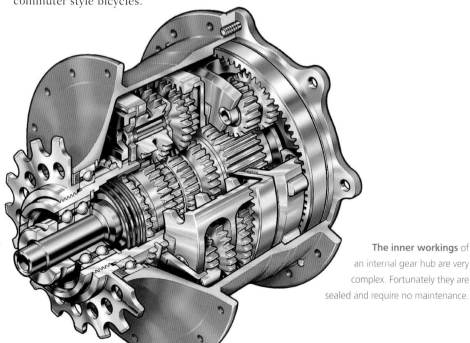

The inner workings of an internal gear hub are very complex. Fortunately they are sealed and require no maintenance.

CHAPTER 6

Fix It

In general, you can choose between a do-it-yourself or a do-it-for me approach to bike maintenance and repair. There are, however, a handful of basic skills you must develop (unless you happen to have a ride-along bike mechanic who tails you everywhere). First and foremost, you need to know how to pump up your bike tires and lube the chain. Beyond that, if your rides are never longer than a mile or two from home, you might never need to handle your own repairs. If your bike breaks down, walk it home and haul it in to your local bike shop. However, should you regularly venture further afield, knowing how to fix a flat tire is a very good skill. And bringing along the equipment to fix said flat is good, as well. Of course, with today's communications connectivity, it is unlikely that you would have to walk ten miles back home because you have had a flat. That is, unless your friends won't take your call…

Knowing how to make basic fit adjustments is helpful. You really don't need to run to the bike shop to have them raise or lower your seat, though they should handle fit for you if they sold you the bike.

Some bicycles have been developed to minimize the amount of maintenance and repair work necessary. Sealed, internal gear hubs never need to be lubricated and have a very long (years and miles) lifespan. Sealed bottom brackets and headsets are nearly impervious to normal exposure.

Your bike should never squeak, clunk, squeal, or creak. The only sound should be the chain clicking softly over the gear teeth and the wheels rolling along. Keep the chain oiled. If people can hear you coming due to your squeaky chain, you are ruining your equipment and working too hard. Squealing brakes, clunking bottom brackets, and creaky crankarms should be inspected and tended to by your local bike mechanic.

• TOOLS AND SUPPLIES

Most bicycle adjustments can be done with screwdrivers, hex wrenches, and box or adjustable wrenches (note that most bikes use metric sizing, so your trusty old set of SAE wrenches might not work really well). Specialized tools are available to fit pedals, bottom brackets, and bearing cone nuts; to remove cassette clusters; to cut cable housings and cut and pull cable; to assist in wheel truing; and to hold a bike in place while it is being serviced. Unless you decide to delve deeply into maintenance and repair (and that happens with some frequency), you won't need to purchase most or any of these tools.

There are some bike specific tools that are necessary (or at least very helpful) even if you don't plan to do more than the most basic upkeep repairs:

- A set of tire levers (plastic tools for removing tires) and a patch kit
- A floor pump (most now come with valves for either Presta or Schrader) is vital
- A chain cleaning kit (plastic container with brushes that holds solvent)
- A skinny cassette brush

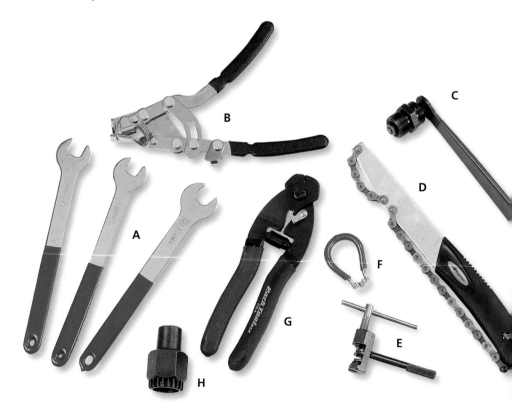

Tools for overhauling bicycles are not that expensive or complicated. A selection of cone wrenches (A), cable puller (B), crankarm extractor (C), chain whip (D), chain breaker (E), spoke wrench (F), cable cutter (G), and bottom bracket tool (H), would get you through most jobs.

• STORING YOUR BICYCLE

How a bicycle is stored affects its longevity and maintenance schedule. The ideal place for bike storage is inside the house, not in the basement. Second choice is inside, in the basement. Third choice is in a totally enclosed garage. Fourth, in a carport. Bicycles that will be stored for more than a month should be hung by the frame, seat post, or both wheels to prevent damage to tires. (Tires always leak slowly, so eventually the bike will have two flat tires and the weight of the bike on flatted tires can ruin the sidewalls.)

Storing a bike so it is exposed directly to the elements is very hard on the machine. The seat will fall apart quickly from exposure to moisture and UV rays in sunlight, so make sure it is always protected. The chain will need to be lubricated after every rain, and the brake and derailleur cables should be lubed weekly on a bike stored outdoors. Sun will cause dry rot in the tires. High-heat, high-sun-intensity locations degrade tires rapidly. Salty air is also very hard on bikes. If you must store your bike outdoors, or you are touring and camping, cover the bike with a tarp.

Bicycle Storage

Slat-wall storage systems for garages and basements usually offer hardware designed specifically for bicycle storage.

• BASIC BICYCLE MAINTENANCE AND REPAIR

The how-tos included here cover the most essential maintenance and adjustment fixes. If you want to get more involved with bicycle repair, many continuing education centers and bike associations offer regular classes. You'll also find that most dedicated cyclists are more than willing to share some information and advice. The great part about bicycles is that you can completely overhaul many bikes with a dozen or so specialized bike tools. No computers necessary!

Repair and maintenance begins with getting your bike properly adjusted to fit your body and your riding habits.

Set Seat Height

The height of the seat is important to riding comfort and efficiency. The seat should be high enough that the knee is almost fully extended on the down stroke. The rider's hips should not rock back and forth while riding—this means the seat is too high.

How to Determine Proper Seat Height and Position

1 The toe test. When the seat is at the right height, you should be able to sit on the seat and just touch the ground with your tiptoes

2 The pedal test. Put your foot flat on the pedal. When the pedal is at the lowest point in its revolution, your leg should be fully extended and your foot should remain flat on the pedal. Have a helper steady the bike for you.

3 The plumb bob test. Suspend a plumb bob (any small, heavy object tied to string will do) downward with the string held next to your knee. Ideally, when the pedals are parallel to the ground (3 o'clock and 9 o'clock position) your knee and the pedal axle should be on the same vertical line. Have a helper steady the bike for you.

Adjust Seat Height

Seat with a quick-release lever. Release the cam lever. Pull up or push down on the seat to adjust the height. Do not pull the seat post out beyond the maximum mark on the post. Make sure the seat is aligned with the top tube and reclamp the cam lever.

TIP

The seat post has a minimum insertion mark beyond which the seat should not be extended.

Seat with a binder bolt and clamp. Use the appropriate tool (usually a hex wrench or an Allen wrench) to loosen the bolt that secures the seat post clamp. Pull up or push down on the seat to adjust the height. Do not pull the seat post out beyond the maximum mark on the post. Make sure the seat is aligned with the top tube and then tighten the binder bolt.

Seat with an old-style binder bolt. Loosen the bolt head with a box (open-end) wrench of the same size. Do not use pliers or clamping pliers. You may need to secure the nut on the other end of the bolt. A box wrench is best for this too, but you may use a clamping pliers as long as you are not attempting to spin with the pliers (this will strip the nut or bolt head). Pull up or push down on the seat to adjust the height. Do not pull the seat post out beyond the maximum mark on the post. Make sure the seat is aligned with the top tube and then tighten the binder bolt.

How to Adjust the Seat Forward/Back and Adjust Tilt

To move the seat forward or back, loosen the hex bolt under the saddle slightly. (Do not take this bolt out unless you are replacing the saddle.) Move the seat forward or backward as needed.

While the seat bolt is loose, you can also adjust the saddle tilt. The saddle should be exactly parallel to the ground—check with a bubble level if you want total accuracy.

Variation: On older bikes, the seat rail clamps are tightened with a binder bolt. Use a box wrench (or a pair of them if the bolt is secured with a nut) to loosen the bolt.

TIP

Prevent Sticking

The seat post often sticks in the seat tube. To prevent this, grease the post annually with lithium grease or anti-seize compound.

How to Make Other Adjustments

How to replace a saddle. The saddle attaches to the seat post via rails and a clamp. To replace the saddle, remove the hex bolt under the saddle. Remove the clamp and remove the saddle. Place the new saddle into the grooves, replace the clamp and thread and tighten the hex bolt. Adjust the seat forward or back, and adjust the tilt as needed. On older bikes, remove the binder bolt with a box wrench.

How to adjust the handlebar height or reach. For fully adjustable handlebars, loosen the hex bolts at both adjustment points and move the stem to the desired location. Tighten the bolts.

How to loosen a threaded headset. Older model bikes with threaded headset and a quill stem have a bolt at the top. Loosen, with three or four turns, (do not remove!) the hex bolt at the center top of the stem. Pull the handlebars back and forth to loosen the stem in the fork.

TIP

If the stem inside the fork is frozen even after you loosen the stem bolt, rap it gently with a rubber mallet or a piece of wood. This should free it up so you can make your handlebar adjustment and then tighten the stem bolt again. Do not pull the stem out beyond the maximum mark indicated on the stem.

How to Replace Handlebar Tape on Drop Style Handlebars

1 Pull back the rubber brake hoods and remove the old handlebar tape by unwrapping it. Most drop handlebars have end caps filling the open ends of the steel tube. Remove these (there may be a set screw in the middle of the cap). Place a 3 to 4 inch piece of handle bar tape around the brake clamps.

2 Remove a small section of the paper covering the adhesive on the handlebar tape. Starting at the open bar end, make the first wrap with about ½ inch hanging over the end of the bar. Wrap the tape clockwise on the right side of the bar and counterclockwise on the left side of the bar. The adhesive strip should be contacting the bar, not overlapping on the tape below it.

3 Continue wrapping the tape around the bar and around the brake body. Stop when you get to the lip in the handlebar. Cut the tape at an angle to match the lip. Secure the end of the handlebar tape with three or four turns of colored or black electrical tape. Flip the brake clamp covers back into position and reattach the end caps.

Replacing Upright Handlebar Grips

Upright handlebar grips get sticky and dirty after a few years. They are very easy to replace. Cut the old grips off the handlebars with a utility knife, or just pull them off if they slide easily. Buy the proper size replacement grips. Spray a squirt or two of hairspray into a grip and quickly slide it onto the handlebar. Make sure you line up any pattern as desired; you have about a minute before the hairspray dries.

Removing Wheels

Because the tire is typically wider than the wheel rim, you need to release the brakes before you can remove a wheel. If you don't release the brakes, the brake pads will prevent the wheel from being removed, as they are spaced closely to the rims.

How to Release Brakes

Cantilever brakes. Pinch the lever arms together at the top and remove the straddle wire cable.

Linear pull brakes. Pinch the lever arms together at the top and lift the metal tube (noodle) out of the linkage bracket.

Side pull or dual pivot caliper brakes: Rotate the brake quick release arm upward. Some brakes of this type may have a button on the brake lever.

Removing a Front Wheel (See Previous Page for Removing Brakes)

Quick-release hubs. Pull on the cam lever to release. Loosen the quick-release nut until the wheel can slip out of the forks. Pull the wheel out. Some bikes have a clip that prevents the wheel from falling out if the quick-release has not been engaged. Pry this clip up to remove the wheel.

Hub with axle nuts. On a non-quick-release wheel, loosen the axle nuts on both sides. One or both sides may have a washer with a hook that clips into the fork. Loosen the nuts enough to disengage the hooks. Do not remove the nuts all the way.

Replacing a Front Wheel

Slide the wheel all the way into the fork drop outs. Make sure the wheel is pushed all the way into the fork drop outs and is centered. The quick-release cam lever is on the non-gear side of the bike.

Quick-release hubs. With the cam lever open, tighten the quick-release nut until it makes light contact with the drop outs. Push the cam lever closed. It should require a moderate amount of effort to push the cam lever all the way closed. If you can't push it all the way closed, release the cam lever and loosen the quick-release nut slightly and try again. Re-engage the brake calipers. For bolted hubs: if present, hook the washer hooks into the holes in the fork. Tighten both nuts equally to secure the wheel between the fork arms. Re-engage the brake calipers.

Removing a Back Wheel

Bike with a coaster brake. The coaster brake has a brake arm or torque arm, which is attached to the left chain stay with a strap and a bolt. Remove the bolt to release the torque arm. After removing the brake arm, loosen the axle bolts and push the axle forward out of the dropouts.

Bike with three-speed internal hub gear. Do not loosen the small wheel on the gear cable. Unscrew the adjuster barrel until the cable disconnects. Loosen the bolts. Push the axle forward out of the dropouts.

Bike with a rear derailleur. Shift gears so the chain is on the smallest cog. Release the rear brake (see page 107). Release the quick-release cam lever (or axle nuts on a non-quick release). Push or pull the derailleur cage back. Push the wheel forward so it slides out of the drop outs. It may take some wiggling back and forth to get the wheel to drop out of forks.

TIP

Protect Your Hands
Removing the back wheel is trickier than the front, as there is usually gearing of some sort to deal with. This can be a dirty job, so wearing latex gloves is a good protective measure if you don't want greasy hands.

How to Remove an Inner Tube

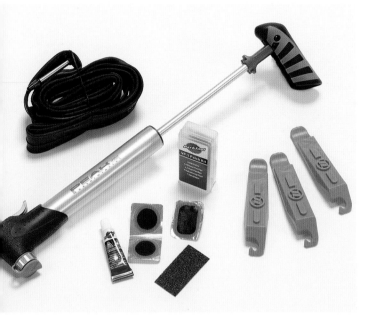

1 Assemble your equipment and supplies. To fix a flat you will need a pump, tire levers, and either a new tube or a patch kit.

2 Remove the wheel from the bike (see pages 106 to 109). If the tube is a Presta tube, remove the valve nut.

3 Starting opposite the valve, push the tire toward the middle of the rim. Slip the smooth end of a tire lever under the bead of the tire.

4 Push down on the lever to pry the tire bead over the wheel rim. Hook the end of the tire lever around a spoke.

5 Move about four or five inches away from the first lever and insert a second lever. Pry the tire bead over the rim and hook the lever to a spoke.

6 Repeat with a third lever. (The second lever will drop out at this time.)

7 The tire should now be loose enough that you can run the tire lever around the entire tire and lift it over the rim.

8 Remove the inner tube. It is not necessary to remove the tire except to fully inspect the inner lining of the tire and to inspect the rim tape.

9 To remove the valve, push the tire back over the rim so you can pull the valve straight out to remove it.

How to Patch an Inner Tube

1 Find the leak. Pump the inner tube up to about twice its normal size. Typically you will hear the hiss of the leak; if you are lucky it will be easily visible. If not, you'll have to submerge the partially inflated tube in water and feed it through as you look for air bubbles.

2 Once you have located the leak, deflate the tube and mark the leak by holding your thumb directly over the hole and then looping the tube under your index finger and pinkie, and over your middle two fingers. If you are at home, you can use a marker to mark crosshatches—but they need to be at least an inch away from the hole so they do not interfere with the patch glue.

3 Using the sandpaper or metal scarifier included in the patch kit, sand around the hole. Make sure to sand an area slightly bigger than the patch. Wipe off the sanding residue.

4 Apply the vulcanizing formula to the area and allow to dry. NOTE: Some patches come with a self-adhesive backing and do not require vulcanizing or cement.

5 Pull the tinfoil backing off the patch. Place the patch over the vulcanized hole. Using the smooth end of a tire lever, push from the center of the patch out toward the edges all over the patch. Use the patch kit box as a hard surface to push against. Make sure all the edges adhere firmly. The plastic patch cover will come off as you do this. Before reinserting the tube, everything must be dry, not sticky.

How to Install an Inner Tube

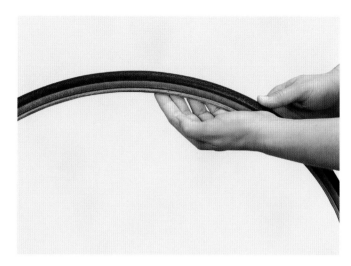

1 Before reinserting the tube, very carefully run your fingers around the inside of the tire to feel for any sharp objects that may have caused the puncture. Take your time, as you do not want to repeat this process five miles down the road. Also, visually inspect the rim tape to see that it is intact and no spoke ends are poking through.

2 If you have removed the tire, replace one side. Inflate the tube very slightly. Reinsert the valve into the rim hole. Tuck the tube back into the tire, taking care not to twist the tube and making sure that it is evenly arranged.

3 Starting at the valve, push the tire bead back over the rim. This is easy until you get to the last few inches. Use the thumbs of both hands to push it into place. If you absolutely cannot place it with your thumbs, use a tire lever to pry it back on. Make sure you aren't pinching the tube with the lever, or you will cause a new hole.

4 Make sure the valve is perfectly upright, and pump up the tire slightly. Check that the valve is still upright. Pinch the tire all around and look to see that the tube is not visible. On a Presta valve, replace the valve nut. Fully inflate the tube (see next page).

Inflating a Tire

Bicycle tires are marked on the sidewall with the proper inflation pressure. Use a pump with an integrated pressure gauge, or use a special bike tire pressure gauge to determine pressure. Proper inflation is very important to prevent flats and to get the most wear possible from a tire. Do not use a gas station air hose to fill your bike tires. The volume of air they produce is suitable for car tires, not bike tires.

It is very easy to damage a valve stem when using a frame pump because you are pushing against the pump, which is directly attached to the valve with no hose to buffer movement. Hold your hand around the rim and behind the pump head to minimize movement and protect the valve.

How to Inflate a Tire

Presta valve. Remove the plastic protective cap. Unscrew the nut on the valve stalk and push it in to release a little pressure. Push the pump head onto the valve all the way. If the head has a flip lock, engage it. Begin pumping. If no air seems to be entering the tire, push the pump head down more. Often you will hear a little pop when the valve releases and air can begin entering the tube. Inflate the tire. Unlock the lock and pull the pump head off the valve. Spin the knob back down tight. Replace the cap.

Schrader valve. Remove the plastic protective cap. Push the pump head onto the valve and flip down the lever to lock. Pump up the tire. Flip up the lever and remove the pump head. Replace the cap.

Adjust Your Brakes

If you can pull the brake levers all the way to the handlebars, either your brake cables need to be tightened or your brake pads are completely worn away. If you can still pull the levers all the way to the handlebars, it is time to take the bike to the bike shop.

Cantilever and direct pull brakes. A barrel adjustment nut is located at the brake lever. Turning this nut counterclockwise will tighten the brake cable.

Caliper brakes. The barrel nut is located at the brake itself. Again, turn counterclockwise to tighten the cable.

TIP: On some newer, high end MTB brakes you can adjust the reach of the brake lever so it is comfortable for you to ride with two fingers always on the levers. Check your owner's manual. The adjustment screw is located just under the barrel nut of the cable adjuster.

TIP: Rotate the brake and gear shifters to the most comfortable position for good riding posture. The hex nut closest to the handlebars is usually the clamp nut. Loosen slightly and rotate to the desired position.

Tools and supplies needed for chain cleaning are a chain scrubber, gear brush, degreaser, chain lube, and rags.

WARNING!

Do not use gasoline or kerosene to clean chains. They are excellent solvents, but they are also explosively flammable and environmentally unfriendly.

Clean and Lube the Chain

Wiping the chain down regularly is a good idea. Occasionally, cleaning the chain will remove the grit that a wipe-down doesn't get. A chain-scrubbing tool makes this job easier. If you don't use a chain scrubber, drape the bike and the surrounding area with plastic and use a toothbrush and solvent to scrub each chain link. This is extremely messy and not terribly effective. Some cyclists remove the chain and soak it in solvent. Repeated removal weakens chains and is time consuming, and this process does not necessarily yield a cleaner chain.

There are a number of scrubbers on the market. These directions are for the Park Tools Cyclone Chain Scrubber (See Resources, page 125).

How to Clean & Lube a Chain

1 Before cleaning the chain, use a gear cleaning brush to clean out the gunk between and on the sprockets. Use a rag to wipe all the accumulated dirt from the sprocket teeth and from the chainring teeth. Also clean the accumulated dirt from the pulley wheels of the rear derailleur.

2 Pull a rag between each layer of sprockets to remove dirt loosened by brush.

3 Take the lid off the chain scrubber and place it under the chain, pushing the chain down into the roller. Put on the lid and snap up the metal clips.

4 Fill the scrubber with solvent to the marked line (do not dilute the solvent). Turn the pedals slowly backwards. The chain will be pulled through the scrubber brushes and solvent. Place a rag under the scrubber opening to catch drips. Make sure to dispose of solvent properly.

5 Clean the scrubber and fill it with soapy water. Run the chain through again. Finally, rinse with clean water. Wipe the chain dry with a rag. To ensure the chain is completely dry, use a hairdryer.

6 Lube the chain by placing a drop of lube on each roller and each rivet.

7 Wipe off the derailleurs and lubricate at the springs and pivot points each time you clean the chain.

Adjusting and Maintaining Derailleurs

If your chain is regularly being pushed off the front chainrings, the limit adjustment on the derailleur needs to be tweaked. If these adjustments don't fix the problem, it is likely that the cable needs adjusting or possibly replacing. Rear derailleurs are trickier to adjust. Shifting problems can be very complex, so it is usually easiest to take the bike to a bike shop for diagnosis.

You're cruising along, you shift gears and your chain drops off. Getting it back on will dirty your fingers, but there is a trick to minimizing the grime. If this happens more than once in a great while, the derailleur needs to be adjusted.

If the chain has come off the front, lift the chain up and place it on top of the smallest chainring, then rotate the pedals forward. The pedaling action will seat the chain on the chainring.

If the chain has come off the back and is jammed either between the cog and the spokes or the cog and the frame, probably the best option is to remove the back wheel.

Working with Derailleurs

If the chain is being pushed off the outside of the large chainring, tighten the high limit (H) screw on the front derailleur, one quarter turn at a time. This is usually the outermost of the two adjustment screws. The space between the inner side of the outside of the derailleur cage should be 1 mm from the chain. If the chain is being dropped off the inside of the small chainring, adjust the low limit (L) screw on the front derailleur. The inner side of the inside of the derailleur cage should be 1 mm from the chain.

If the chain has come off the front, lift the chain up and place it on top of the smallest chainring, then rotate the pedals forward. The pedaling action will seat the chain on the chainring.

BICYCLE MAINTENANCE SCHEDULE

How often to maintain a bike is partially dependent upon the type of bike, type of riding, and the weather conditions. Off road bikes used in muddy, sandy, dusty, and salty conditions will need to be cleaned and lubed much more often than comfort bikes ridden low miles in nice weather. High performance bicycles need to have drivetrain parts (chain, chainrings, and cassettes) changed fairly often. Utility bikes with sturdy chains and internal gear hubs will rarely need drivetrain replacement.

Check the crankarms regularly. There should be no play or looseness. If there is, the bottom bracket needs adjusting or replacement.

As with everything else, there are a thousand different opinions and recommendations for when to replace parts and overhaul bearings. When looking at recommendations, it is good to know the riding parameters. Of course, racers of any sort will be replacing the drive train (chainrings, cassette, and chain) every 2,000 to 3,000 miles. Their race performance depends upon peak output. On the other hand, cycle tourists are not likely to stop and overhaul their bikes halfway through their cross-country tour. Many people are riding bikes that haven't been maintained in years. Though these bikes work, they are probably inefficient and likely potentially dangerous.

Here is a very basic maintenance schedule applicable to average riders under average conditions.

Before Every Ride

- Check tire pressure
- Check that quick releases on wheels and seat are tightly closed
- Pull brakes tight—levers should not contact handlebars; tighten cables if necessary
- Release brakes—pads should be an equal distance from rims

After Every Ride

- Check tire condition (look for cuts in tread or bead wall)
- Wash and dry if ridden in mud or rain
- Lube chain if ridden in rain or after washing

Every 500 Miles or Annually

- Clean and lubricate chain
- Lubricate pivot points and brake and derailleur cables
- Check that wheels are true (spin the wheels and look for wiggles or wobbles)
- Check bottom bracket tightness (pull and push side to side on crankarms to see if there is looseness in bottom bracket)
- Check wheel hub tightness (pull wheel side to side to see if there is looseness in the hub bearings)
- Check all bolts for tightness (handlebar, stem, seat post, chainring, bottle cage, rack mounts, derailleur mounts, cable anchors, and racks)

If wheels are out of true or bottom bracket or hubs are loose, take the bike in to be repaired as soon as possible.

Every 5000 Miles or Annually if Ridden in Wet Conditions

- Overhaul or replace bearings in bottom bracket, headset, wheel hubs, and pedals
- Replace brake and derailleur cables and housings

You can learn how to perform these tasks at some bike shops or at community education programs.

APPENDIX: Cycling Fun & Adventure Guide

It may be that the limit of your cycling is short hops to the grocery store or transit station. The biking bug may bite, however, and you may discover that cycling is absolutely the most fun ever and you want to do more of it. Fortunately, there really is no limit to the amount of cycling you can do. Instead of biking to the transit stop, you can bike your whole commute. You can pop the bike on your car rack and drive to a beautiful rail trail and go for a long, peaceful ride. In most areas there are bike clubs for riders of all sorts. If you are competitive, there are races for every bike made and every imaginable rider, as well. You could even make your next vacation a bike-centric trip. The options are truly amazing.

Many areas now have bike racks on buses and hanging hooks in train cars to allow for more transportation options.

LONG DISTANCE COMMUTES

The two mile ride to the bus stop doesn't seem like a ride at all. How about riding the entire commute? This, of course, is dependent on many variables. If your commute is thirty miles each direction, that would be a lot of biking. Some urban areas just don't have good routes for biking from suburbs to city center or from suburb to suburb. But there are some options.

If the commuting distance is too long to comfortably complete before work, or to complete both ways, think about a one-way trip. In many areas buses have bike racks (they usually only hold two bikes, unfortunately) and commuter trains have bike hooks or bike cars. You can take your bike to work via transit, then bike home the entire way. This also solves the issue of arriving at work hot and sweaty. Biking home is a great way to decompress after work.

Another option is to look for transit stops that are easily accessible by bike, but are farther away. Maybe that two mile ride can become a five mile ride.

Finally, you may get to a level where you can ride a twenty or thirty mile commute. Many serious cyclists use their commute as a training ride. It's certainly possible, and definitely something to aspire to.

RACING

Amateur cycle racing is divided into age and skill categories, so you are competing against cyclists of your level. There are a number of different types of bicycle races for many types of bicycles. A time trial is a race against the clock. Cyclists enter the course at regular intervals, so they are riding alone, and the object is to make the best time. Criterium (crit) races are run around a short loop, usually one to two miles. Crit races test the rider's ability to ride fast in a tight pack and corner well. In professional crit races, prizes are given at intervals throughout the race for the first rider to pass the start/finish line. These prizes encourage much jockeying for position and sprinting. These races are very popular because it is easy to set up the short loop without closing many streets, and the cycling action is very spectator friendly because of the sprinting and how often the cyclists pass by. A road race is a long distance race, usually out on country roads. The riders all start at the same time, and the first rider across the line wins. Road races can range up to 100 miles or more. A stage race is a series of races that takes place over a number of days. Stage races usually include road races and time trials.

Racing opportunities exist for all types of bikes. Road bike races include time trials, criteriums, and road races. Mountain bike races include downhill, slalom, cross-country, and hill climb. BMX races are held on short tracks with jumps and moguls. Cyclocross events are usually held in the winter or rainy season, and are meant to test the riders' ability to overcome obstacles and slippery conditions. Dismounting and carrying the bike is a part of cyclocross racing. Track racing is done with a special track bike at a banked bike track called a velodrome. There are numerous types of track races.

Amateur bike races, like this road race, happen every weekend.

Track racing on a velodrome develops a whole new level of cycling skills and tactical techniques.

Joining a cycling club is a great way to socialize and have fun on your bike.

You can see the world in a very special way on a bicycle.

JOIN A CLUB

There are thousands of bicycling clubs throughout the country. You can find clubs that cater to older riders, slower riders, racers, women, singles, recumbent cyclists, tourists, off road riders, tandem cyclists—you name it and you can probably find a cycling club. Internet searches and inquiries at your local bike shops will generate many leads. Almost every state has a cycling association which sponsors races, or a statewide consortium of cycling groups.

Most clubs have regular rides—usually weekly—and special weekend or event rides. Club rides are great ways to meet other cyclists and improve your cycling skills. Or your tire changing skills. It is inevitable that you will get a flat on your first ride with a club. Make sure your tire repair skills are up to snuff and you have the equipment you need to fix a flat. Before showing up for a club ride, contact the club to find out how they handle new members. Many racing clubs have special novice or new member rides to determine where you might fit. It is always better to underestimate your ability in these cases. Some groups are very welcoming and tolerant of novices, and some are not.

BIKING VACATIONS

People have taken cycling vacations everywhere in the world (except perhaps Antarctica—though one south pole scientist does use his folding bike to ride between test sites). You can do a self-guided tour and carry all your own gear and camp overnight, or you can pay a bicycle touring company to map your route and arrange luxury accommodations at every turn. Options exist for every point in between these extremes. Many books have been published outlining daytrips, and weeklong or longer tours. Many well-established bike-touring companies offer tours almost anywhere you would care to ride a bike. You can choose a tour that focuses on history or wine tasting or natural scenery. Adventure Cycling has researched many cross country bike routes and sells detailed maps with cycle appropriate roads marked, as well as amenities such as campgrounds, hotels, restaurants, grocery stores, and bike shops.

RIDE AN EVENT TOUR

On every weekend during bicycling weather (and non-cycling weather!) you can find a charity bike tour somewhere in the U.S. The two-day, 150-mile ride is very popular, as are the one-day century (100 mile) rides. These events can be huge, with 5,000 or more participants. Usually an entry fee is required, as well as a collection of a set dollar amount of donations. The group organizes pit stops with food and water, and sometimes mechanics and entertainment, as well as overnight accommodations and transportation from finish to start (if not a loop route). A sag wagon is available if you cannot ride the whole route.

Some cities sponsor bicycle tour days when city streets are closed off to traffic. For a fee you can ride around town without concern for cars or trucks running you down. These rides often feature entertainment every few miles and lots of handouts from food and beverage vendors. These are great rides for families to do together.

Not all tours are fundraisers, and some are weeklong events. The most famous of these is RAGBRAI (Register's Annual Great Bike Ride Across Iowa). Ten thousand riders ride across Iowa in a weeklong event that highlights the beauty and charm of this Midwestern state. Many other states have now followed suit, and you can find a number of weeklong rides that crisscross a state. Many of the tours have smaller limit numbers, as low as 40 or 50, so the crowds are not as overwhelming. Tours usually average 50 to 80 miles per day depending upon terrain.

Almost every state has numerous charity bike rides. Ride with a team to increase your fun.

Bicycle touring is a great way to slow down and visit destinations all over the world.

Glossary

bonk: depletion of glycogen stores resulting in inability to function physically or mentally

boot: a temporary patch placed on a punctured tire to protect the tube

brakehoods: the rubber covers over the brake lever mechanism on drop handlebars

braze-ons: the threaded pegs on bike frames to attach bottle cages, racks, or other accessories

bunny hop: lifting both wheels off the ground to clear an obstacle

cadence: speed of pedaling

campy: nickname for Campagnolo, the premier component manufacturer

century: 100 miles; metric century, 100 kilometers or 62 miles

cleat: the fastening mechanism that attaches to the shoe in clipless pedal systems

clincher: the standard wire or Kevlar beaded tire

clipless: a pedal and cleat system that latches the shoe to the pedal without use of toe clips or cages

criterium (crit): a bike race that goes around many laps on a short course

dab: to touch the ground with your foot

dialed in: describes a bike that fits perfectly or ride or race that was perfect

dish: the offsetting of the rear right side spokes to allow room for the cassette

draft: riding in the slipstream of the rider ahead

dropouts: the slots on frame and fork into which the wheel axles slide

drops: the lower part of drop style handlebars

endo: flying over the front handlebars while the bike goes end over end

face plant: when the rider's face hits the ground after an endo

fit kit: a set of measuring tools that bike shops use to optimize bike fit

fixed gear (fixie): a single gear bike with no coaster mechanism

granny gear: very small chainring or very low gear

gruppo: a complete set of components by the same manufacturer

hammer (or mash): to ride hard in a high gear

hardtail: a mountain bike with no rear suspension

knobby: tires with large blocky tread

LBS: local bike shop

masterlink: a special chain link that is used to break the chain rather than pushing out a rivet

peleton: the main group of cyclists in a race

road rash: the wound resulting from flesh dragged across a road surface

sag wagon: a vehicle that follows a group of riders to pick up those who need assistance

singletrack: a bike trail wide enough for a single bike

snakebite: a tire flat caused when the tube is pinched by the rim; it looks like two holes caused by snake fangs

spin: to maintain a high cadence

squirrel: a rider who cannot maintain a straight line or is unpredictable

taco (pretzel or potato chip): to bend a wheel

technical: a trail or route that requires a high level of skill
to traverse

track stand: balancing the bike while still with both feet on the pedals

travel: the maximum length of movement on a suspension system

velodrome: a bicycle racing track, usually with steeply banked curves

Resources

The bicycle manufacturers on this list produce all sorts of bicycles. With the exception of some custom manufacturers, all sell at least some bicycles under $1200. There are dozens of bicycle touring and bicycle advocacy groups. Only a small sample are listed here.

Bicycle Manufacturers

Bacchetta Recumbent Bikes
bacchettabikes.com

Bianchi
bianchiusa.com

Big Cat Human Powered Vehicles
catrike.com

Bike Friday
bikefriday.com

Brompton Bicycle
brompton.co.uk

Cannondale
cannondale.com

Civia
civiacycles.com

Co-Motion Cycles
co-motion.com

Dahon
dahon.com

Diamondback Bicycles
diamondback.com

Electra
electrabike.com

Fuji
fujibikes.com

Giant
giant-bicycles.com

GT Bicycles
gtbicycles.com

Intense
intenseBMX.com

Jamis Bicycles
jamisbikes.com

Kona
konaworld.com

Larry vs Harry
larryvsharry.com

Linus Bikes
linusbike.com

Marin Bikes
marinbikes.com

Masi
masibikes.com

Melon
melonbicycles.com

Mongoose
mongoose.com

Motobecane
motobecane.com

Phat Cycles
phatcycles.com

Public
publicbikes.com

Raleigh
raleighusa.com

Rans
ransbikes.com

Redline
redlinebicycles.com

Rivendell Bicycle Works
rivbike.com

Rohloff
rohloff.de

Salsa
salsacycles.com

Santa Cruz
santacruzbicycles.com

Santana
santanatandem.com

Schwinn
schwinnbike.com

Scott
scott-sports.com

Specialized
specialized.com

Sun
sunbicycles.com

Surly
surlybikes.com

Swobo
swobo.com

Terry Precision Cycling
terrybicycles.com

Torker
torkerusa.com

Trek
trekbikes.com

Univega
univega.com

Waterford Precision Cycles
waterfordbikes.com

Clothing, Accessories, and Tools

Bike Nashbar
bikenashbar.com

Performance Bicycle
performancebike.com

BikeBagShop.com
bikebagshop.com

Gear Up
sportssolutions.com

Pearl Izumi
shop.pearlizumi.com

REI
rei.com

Road ID
roadid.com

Park Tool
parktool.com

Bicycle Touring

Adventure Cycling Association
adventurecycling.org

WomanTours
womantours.com

Freewheeling Adventures
freewheeling.ca

Backroads
backroads.com

Bike MS
nationalmssociety.org

Other sites of interest

League of American Bicyclists
bikeleague.org

Utility Cycling
utilitycycling.org

Pedestrian and Bicycling Information Center
bicyclinginfo.org

Credits

Shutterstock, pp. 4, 6 top left, 9 top and bottom right, 10 right, 14, 15 left, 24, 29, 33 left, 34, 35 left, 39 right, 44, 49 left, 52, 54 right, 55, 59, 61, 62 left, 63 top right and bottom middle, 64 both, 68 both, 70 left, 71 right, 74 left, 75 right, 80 all, 86 left, 120 both, 121 right, 122 bottom.

Dennis Hallinan/Getty Images, p. 5.

iStockphoto, pp. 6 all except top left, 10 left, 11 bottom, 15 middle and right, 33 right, 35 right, 36, 38 both, 39 left, 40 right, 50, 53 top, 54 left, 58, 63 all except top right and bottom middle, 77 bottom, 78, 79 both, 86 right, 87, 95 left.

Photolibrary, (Joerg Reuther) p. 11 top, (Marcos Welsh) p. 40 left, (Ingram Publishing) p. 53 bottom, (Peter Burian) p. 121 left, (Lothar Schulz) p. 122 top, (Stella Stella) p. 123 right.

Contributors

Civia Cycles, Page 21, lower right, www.civiacycles.com, 952 229 5040

Garmin International, Page 32, www.garmin.com, 913 397 8200

Gear Up, Inc., Page 101, left, www.mygearup.com, 800 346 7332

Marin Bikes, Page 21, middle right, www.marinbikes.com, 415 382 6000

Phat Cycles/Cycle Support West, Inc., www.phatcycles.com, 877 884 7428

Renee Ridenour, Page 123, left, Photosbyrenee.smugmug.com, 302 836 3861

Salsa Cycles, Salsa Chili Con Crosso, www.salsacycles.com, 877 668 6223

Specialized Bicycles, Page 20, left, www.specialized.com, 408 779 6229

VSI Products, Inc., Page 23, top, www.vsiproducts.com, 562 407 2184

Index